William Richard Le Fanu

Seventy Years of Irish Life

Anecdotes And Reminiscences

William Richard Le Fanu

Seventy Years of Irish Life
Anecdotes And Reminiscences

ISBN/EAN: 9783744713696

Printed in Europe, USA, Canada, Australia, Japan

Cover: Foto ©ninafisch / pixelio.de

More available books at **www.hansebooks.com**

SEVENTY YEARS OF IRISH LIFE.

SEVENTY YEARS OF IRISH LIFE

BEING

ANECDOTES AND REMINISCENCES.

BY

W. R. LE FANU.

LONDON:
EDWARD ARNOLD,
37, BEDFORD STREET, STRAND, W.C.
Publisher to the India Office.
1893.

LONDON:
PRINTED BY WILLIAM CLOWES AND SONS, LIMITED,
STAMFORD STREET AND CHARING CROSS.

TO HER

WHOSE LOVE AND GOODNESS

HAVE MADE MY LIFE

THE HAPPY ONE IT HAS BEEN,

TO MY WIFE,

WITH GRATEFUL HEART,

I DEDICATE THIS BOOK.

PREFACE.

It requires no ordinary amount of courage, even in an author of established fame, to come before the public when he has long passed the age of threescore years and ten; yet here am I, who never wrote a line for publication, and never meant to do so, daring to make my first attempt in my eight and seventieth year. I should not have had the courage to venture on such an undertaking, had I not been urged by literary friends (who ought to have known better) to jot down some recollections of my earlier days, and to publish some of the Irish stories which from time to time, in my long life, I have heard.

In politics I have never taken any part, and I have tried, I hope successfully, to keep clear of them in what I have written.

I trust I have said nothing to hurt the feelings of any of my fellow-countrymen; and I leave it to a generous public to pardon the many faults and shortcomings of my first and only book.

W. R. LE FANU.

SUMMERHILL, ENNISKERRY,
October, 1893.

CONTENTS.

CHAPTER I.

Early days—A royal visit to Ireland in 1820 : Grattan's witticism—A maid for a dog—A disciple of Isaak Walton as preceptor—Sheridan Le Fanu's youthful verses and relaxations—A parrot at prayers; and a monkey with the parrot 1

CHAPTER II.

Lord Edward Fitzgerald's dagger—United Irishmen: the apologia of John Sheares—Doctor Dobbin's kind deeds—The story of the Ilchester oak—An outlaw sportsman: his narrow escape and sad ending 16

CHAPTER III.

Faction fights: the Reaskawallahs and Coffeys—Paternal chastisement—A doctor in livery—I bear the olive branch—Battles of the buryings—Dead men's shoes—Fairy doctors: their patient spoils a coachman's toggery—Superstitions about birds 31

CHAPTER IV.

Good will of the peasantry before 1831—A valentine—A justice's bulls—A curious sight indeed—Farms to grow fat on—Some cooks—"What the Dean wears on his legs"—Bloodthirsty gratitude—Old servants and their theories 42

CHAPTER V.

The tithe war of 1831 : the troops come to our village—A marked man—"Push on; they are going to kill ye!"—Not his brother's keeper—Boycotting in the thirties—None so dead as he looked—Lord Cloncurry's manifesto—A fulfilled prophecy 55

CHAPTER VI.

The pleasures of coaching—I enter at Trinity College, Dublin—A miser Fellow: Anecdotes about—Whately, Archbishop of Dublin, and his legs—The vocative of "cat"—Charles Lever's retort-courteous to the Bishop 68

CHAPTER VII.

The "Charleys'" life was not a pleasant one—Paddy O'Neill and his rhymes—"With my rigatooria"—Too far west to wash—On the coast at Kilkee—"Phaudrig Crohoore"—The *Dublin Magazine* ... 81

CHAPTER VIII.

Peasant life after the famine of 1847—An aged goose—Superstitions and Irish peculiarities—The worship of Baal—The Blarney stone—The wren boys—The direful "wurrum"—A remedy for the chin cough, and doctors' remedies 99

CHAPTER IX.

Mitchelstown remembered—A night on the Galtees—The weird horse—Killing or murder?—The ballad of "Shamus O'Brien"—A letter from Samuel Lover 116

CHAPTER X.

A determined duel—I act the peasant, and am selected for the police force—Death of my sister—Sketch of my brother's life—Dan O'Connell's "illustrious kinsman"—A murderous Grand Jury—A sad reflection 130

CHAPTER XI.

The power of the people—Sergeant Murphy; his London manners—Pat Costello's humour—I meet Thackeray—Paddy Blake's echo—Dan O'Connell's imagination—Sir James O'Connell's anecdotes—He is prayed for by his herd 145

CHAPTER XII.

A proselytizing clergyman—Some examples of religious intolerance—An inverse repentance—The true faith—The railway mania—Famine of 1846—Mrs. Norton solves a difficulty—The old Beefsteak Club—A pleasant dinner-party 157

CONTENTS.

CHAPTER XIII.

Smith O'Brien's rebellion—Louis Philippe's interview with the Queen, as seen by the boy Jones—Plain fare and pleasant—Married by mistake—A time for everything—A pagan altar-piece—Drawing the long-bow—Proof against cross-examination—Fooling the English—Larceny or trespass? 170

CHAPTER XIV.

Anthony Trollope: his night encounter—A race for life on an engine—Railway adventures—I become Commissioner of Public Works—Some Irish repartees and ready car-drivers—Rail against road—No cause for uneasiness 190

CHAPTER XV.

Tory Island: its king, customs, and captive—William Dargan: his career and achievements—Agricultural and industrial experiments—Bianconi, the carman—Sheridan Knowles: his absence of mind—Absent-minded gentlemen—Legal complications—Judges and barristers—Lord Norbury 204

CHAPTER XVI.

Irish bulls—Sayings of Sir Boyle Roche—Plutarch's lives—A Grand Jury's decision—Clerical anecdotes and Biblical difficulties—A harmless lunatic—Dangerous recruits—Tom Burke—Some memorials to the Board of Works 224

CHAPTER XVII.

Shooting and fishing—Good snipe grounds—Killarney and Powerscourt—My fishing record—Playing a rock—Salmon flies—Salmon and trout—Grattan's favourites—Hooking a bird—Fishing anecdotes—Lord Spencer's adventure 243

CHAPTER XVIII.

Illicit stills—Getting a reward—Poteen—Past and present—Dress and dwellings—Marriage and language—Material improvement since 1850 272

CHAPTER XIX.

The science of hypnotism—Early experiments and lessons—A drink of cider—I convert Isaac Butt—All wrong—A dangerous power ... 282

CHAPTER XX.

Catholic Emancipation, 1829—The tithe war of 1832—The great famine of 1846—The Fenian agitation of 1865—France against England—Land-hunger—Crime and combination—Last words 292

ILLUSTRATIONS.

PORTRAIT OF W. R. LE FANU ... ... *Frontispiece*
PORTRAIT OF JOSEPH SHERIDAN LE FANU *To face page* 86

SEVENTY YEARS OF IRISH LIFE.

CHAPTER I.

Early days—A royal visit to Ireland in 1821 : Grattan's witticism—A maid for a dog—A disciple of Isaak Walton as preceptor—Sheridan Le Fanu's youthful verses and relaxations—A parrot at prayers; and a monkey with the parrot.

I WAS born on the 24th of February, 1816, at the Royal Hibernian Military School in the Phœnix Park, Dublin; my father being then chaplain to that institution. I was the youngest of three children—the eldest was Catherine Frances; the second, Joseph Sheridan, author of " Uncle Silas," and other novels, and of " Shamus O'Brien " and other Irish ballads.

Here the first ten years of my life were spent, in as happy a home as boy could have. Never can I forget our rambles through that lovely park, the delight we took in the military reviews, sham fights, and races held near the school, not to mention the intense interest and awe inspired by the duels occasionally fought there. The usual time for these hostile meetings was at or soon after daybreak. I only saw one, which from some cause or other took place at a later hour; four shots were fired, after which a reconciliation took place. On more than one such occasion my father acted as peacemaker, and found that the cause of quarrel was something trivial and ridiculous; except by him, there was seldom any interference with these combats. I shall give presently an account of one of the last duels in Ireland, fought about twenty years later.

At an early age my brother gave promise of the powers which he afterwards attained. When between five and six years old a favourite amusement of his was to draw little pictures, and under each he would print some moral which the drawing was meant to illustrate. I well remember one which I specially admired and looked upon as a masterpiece of art, conveying a solemn warning. A balloon was high in air; the two aeronauts had fallen from the boat, and were tumbling headlong to the ground; underneath was printed in fine bold Roman letters, "See the effects of trying to go to heaven." He composed little songs also, which he very sweetly sang, and some old people can still recall his wonderful acting as a mere boy in our juvenile theatricals.

One of my earliest recollections is of the rejoicings, illuminations, and reviews that took place on the accession of George IV. to the throne in 1820, and the excitement caused by his visit to

Ireland in 1821. Royal journeys were not in those days carried out with the ease and celerity with which they are now performed. The king's departure from London, *en route* for Dublin, is thus described in the Annual Register:—

"About half-past eleven o'clock his Majesty left his palace in Pall Mall on his way to Ireland. His Majesty went in his plain dark travelling carriage, attended by Lord Graves, as the lord-in-waiting, escorted by a party of the 14th Light Dragoons. The king proceeded as far as Kingston with his own horses, and from thence to Portsmouth with post-horses. His Majesty was to embark and dine on board the royal yacht."

I saw his state entrance into Dublin from the balcony of my grandfather's house in Eccles Street, through which the procession passed on its way from Howth, where the king had landed. His Majesty was seated in an open carriage drawn by eight splendid horses, and attended by a number of grooms and footmen in magnificent liveries. He was in military uniform, and constantly took off his hat and smiled and bowed gracefully to the people, who enthusiastically cheered him. It was told that a man in the crowd close to the carriage stretched out his hand to the king, saying, "Shake hands, your Majesty." The king at once gave him a hearty shake by the hand. The man then waved his hand, and called out, "Begorra, I'll never wash that hand again!" The king ended a speech which he made to the people from the steps of the Vice-regal Lodge in the following words:—" This is one of the happiest days of my life. I have long wished to visit you; my heart has always been Irish. From the day it first beat I have loved Ireland. This day has shown me that I am beloved by my Irish subjects. Rank, station, honours are nothing; but to feel that I live in the hearts of my Irish subjects is to me the most exalted happiness. I must once more thank you for your kindness, and bid you farewell. Go, and do by me as I shall do by you— drink my health in a bumper. I shall drink all yours in a bumper of Irish whisky." There was a grand review in the Phœnix Park, at which I well remember some of the infantry regiments still wore white knee-breeches and long black gaiters, and nearly all of them very tall shakos, broad at the top, from which rose long feathers, some red and white, some white. After a stay of about three weeks in Ireland, the king embarked for England at Dunleary, then little more than a fishing village, but now, under its new name " Kingstown," which George IV. then gave it, one of the most flourishing towns in Ireland. It was eight and twenty years before Ireland was again visited by an English sovereign.

The enthusiasm awakened by the king's visit soon subsided, and ere long he was no more popular than he had been before. Grattan it was who said that "the Irish abused him in every possible shape.

First, they abused his person, of which he is very vain; secondly, they abused his mistress, of whom he is very fond; and not content with all that, they praised his own wife."

It was shortly after the time I have been speaking of that I met with a rather serious accident, owing to my desire to become possessor of a learned dog. I was about five years old, and, with the children's maid, Maria Walsh, who took care of me, happened to be in our stable-yard when the coachman of Colonel Spottiswoode, the Commandant of the Hibernian School, came into the yard on some message. He had with him a handsome red spaniel, which knew a great number of tricks, all of which the coachman made him perform for me. I was astonished and delighted, and said, "Oh, how I wish I had a dog like that! I'd give anything for a dog like that." "Then," said the man, "you can easily have him. Give me Maria, and I'll give you the dog." "Oh, I'm so glad!" I said. "Take her, take her, and give me the darling dog." He put the dog's chain into my hand, took the girl on his arm, and walked with her out of the yard gate. No sooner had they disappeared than it repented me of what I had done. I burst into floods of tears, and shouted, "Come back, come back! Take your nasty dog, and give me back my own Maria." Getting no answer, I dropped the dog's chain, and ran after the pair as hard as I could run; as I came to the gate I tripped and fell. I was stunned, and my forehead was cut open on the sharp spud stone. The coachman and maid carried me into the kitchen. My sister saw them carrying me in, from a window, and ran down to see what was the matter. She found me with my face covered with blood, ran to the drawing-room, and, not wishing to frighten her mother, called her father out. "Oh, papa," she said, "there's poor little Willie in the kitchen; and I think his eye is hanging down on his cheek!" I wasn't, however, so bad as all that; but, in addition to a bad cut, there was a slight fracture of the frontal bone, and there is still a hollow where it was broken. I never tried to part with Maria again. She did not marry the coachman. What became of him I know not; but she never left me till five and fifty years after, when she died in my house at the age of seventy-five. She was one of the girls brought up at the Hibernian Military School, where there were then two hundred soldiers' daughters, as well as four hundred boys; now the institution is exclusively for boys. Most of these boys become soldiers; their uniform, their drill, their band, as well as the recollection of what their fathers are, or were, makes them long for a military career. Not the least pretty and interesting part of a review in the Phœnix Park, on the Queen's Birthday, is to see these little fellows march past; and how well they march past, led on by their band playing the "British Grenadiers!" From early associations it is to me a very touching sight.

In the year 1826, my father having been appointed Dean of Emly and Rector of Abington, we left Dublin to live at Abington, in the county of Limerick. Here our education, except in French and English, which our father taught us, was entrusted to a private tutor, an elderly clergyman, Stinson by name, who let us learn just as much, or rather as little, as we pleased. For several hours every day this old gentleman sat with us in the schoolroom, when he was supposed to be engaged in teaching us classic lore, and invigorating our young minds by science; but being an enthusiastic disciple of old Isaak, he in reality spent the whole, or nearly the whole, time in tying flies for trout or salmon and in arranging his fishing gear, which he kept in a drawer before him. Soon after he had come to us, he had wisely taken the precaution of making us learn by heart several passages from Greek and Latin authors; and whenever our father's step was heard to approach the schoolroom, the flies were nimbly thrown into the drawer, and the old gentleman, in his tremulous and nasal voice, would say, "Now, Joseph, repeat that ode of Horace," or "William, go on with that dialogue of Lucian." These passages we never forgot, and though more than sixty years have passed, I can repeat as glibly as then the dialogue beginning, $\mathring{\Omega}$ πάτερ οἷα πέπονθα, and others. As soon as our father's step was heard to recede, "That will do," said our preceptor; the drawer was reopened, and he at once returned, with renewed vigour, to his piscatory preparations, and we to our games. Fortunately my father's library was a large and good one; there my brother spent much of his time in poring over many a quaint and curious volume. As for me, under the guidance and instructions of our worthy tutor, I took too ardently to fishing to care much for anything else. I still profit by those early lessons. I can to-day tie a trout or salmon fly as well as most men.

The appearance of our venerable preceptor was peculiar. His face was red, his hair snow-white; he wore, twice-folded round his neck (as the fashion then was), a very high white cravat; his body was enclosed in a bottle-green frock coat, the skirts of which were unusually long; a pair of black knee-breeches and grey stockings completed his costume. In addition to his other accomplishments he was a great performer on the Irish bagpipes, and often after lessons would cheer us with an Irish air, and sometimes with an Irish song. But, alas! how fleeting are all earthly joys; our happy idle days with our reverend friend were soon to cease. My father found that we were learning absolutely nothing, and discovered, moreover, some serious delinquencies on the part of the old gentleman, who was summarily dismissed in disgrace. For some years we did not know what had become of him, and then heard that he had become a violent Repealer, and sometimes marched, playing party tunes on the pipes, at the head of O'Connell's processions. The Repealers were of course delighted to have a Protestant clergyman, no matter how disreputable, in their ranks.

In his old age our quondam tutor led, I fear, a far from reputable life in Dublin. I never saw him but once again. It was many years after he had left us; and oh, what a falling off was there! I beheld my friend, whom I had known as the prince of anglers for trout and salmon, sitting, meanly clad, on the bank of the river Liffey, close to Dublin, engaged in the ignoble sport of bobbing for eels.

When scarcely fifteen years of age my brother Joseph had written many pieces of poetry, which showed a depth of imagination and feeling unusual in a boy of that age. The following are extracts from some of them I have preserved, and which, I think, show remarkable talent for a boy of fifteen years of age :—

> " Oh, lovely moon, so bright and so serene,
>   Rolling thy silver disc so silently,
> Full many an ardent lover's eye, I ween,
>   Rests on thy waning crescent pensively;
> And many an aged eye is fixed on thee
>   That seeks to read the hidden things of fate;
> And many a captive pining to be free,
>   Welcomes thy lustre through his prison gate,
> And feels while in thy beam not quite so desolate.
>
> " There is an hour of sadness all have known,
>   That weighs upon the heart we scarce know why ;
> We feel unfriended, cheerless and alone,
>   We ask no other pleasure but to sigh,

And muse on days of happiness gone by :
  A painful lonely pleasure which imparts
A calm regret, a deep serenity,
  That soothes the rankling of misfortune's darts,
And kindly lends a solace even to broken hearts."

INTRODUCTION TO O'DONOGHUE—AN UNFINISHED POEM.

"Muse of green Erin! break thine icy slumbers,
  Wake yet again thy wreathed lyre ;
Burst forth once more to strike thy tuneful numbers,
  Kindle again thy long extinguished fire.
Long hast thou slept amid thy country's sorrow,
  Darkly thou set'st amid thy country's woes ;
Dawn yet again to cheer a gloomy morrow,
  Break with the spell of song thy long repose.
Why should I bid thee, Muse of Erin, waken?
  Why should I bid thee strike thy harp once more?
Better to leave thee silent and forsaken,
  Than wake thee but thy glory to deplore.
How could I bid thee tell of Tara's towers,
  Where once thy sceptred princes sat in state,
Where rose thy music at the festal hours
  Through the proud halls where listening thousands sat ?
Fallen thy fair castles, past thy princes' glory;
  Thy tuneful bards were banished or were slain ;
Some rest in glory, in their death-beds gory,
  And some have lived to feel a foeman's chain.
Yet for the sake of thine unhappy nation,
  Yet for the sake of Freedom's spirit dead,
Teach thy wild harp to thrill with indignation,
  Peal a deep requiem on her sons that bled.
Yes, like the farewell breath of evening sighing,
  Sweep thy cold hand its silent strings along,
Flash like the lamp beside the hero dying,
  Then hushed for ever be thy plaintive song."

FROM THE SAME.

"I saw my home again at that soft hour
When evening weeps for the departed day,
And sheds her pensive tears on tree and flower,
And sighs her sorrow through the brooklet's spray;
When the sweet thrush pours forth his vesper lay,
When slumber closes every graceful bell,
And the declining sun's last lingering ray
Seems to the fading hills to bid farewell;
And as I looked on this fair scene the big tears fell."

He let no one see these poems but his mother, his sister, and myself. Whether he feared his father's criticism I cannot tell, but he never let him see them; still, he certainly had no great dread of my father, for whenever he had incurred his displeasure he would at once disarm him by some witty saying. One thing that much distressed the Dean was his being habitually late for prayers. One morning breakfast was nearly over and he had not appeared; and when he at last came in it was near ten o'clock. My father, holding his watch in his hand, said in his severest voice, "I ask you, Joseph, I ask you seriously, is this right?" "No, sir," said Joe, glancing at the watch; "I'm sure it must be fast."

Practical jokes, I am glad to say, are seldom practised now, but in my early days they were much in vogue. Here is one my brother played on me:—I was in Dublin, and had a long letter from my father, who was at home at Abington, giving me several commissions. In a postscript, he said, "Send me immediately 'Dodd's Holy Curate.' If Curry has not got it you will be sure to get it at some other booksellers'; but be sure to send it, if possible, by return of post." Curry had it not; in vain I sought it at other booksellers, so I wrote to my father to say that it was not to be had in Dublin, and that Curry did not know the book, but had written to his publishers in London to send it direct to Abington. By return of post I had a letter from my father saying he was utterly at a loss to know what I meant, that he had never asked me to get him "Dodd's Holy Curate," and had never known of the existence of such a book. There is, in fact, no such book. What had happened was this: my father had gone out of the library for a few minutes, and had left his letter to me, which he had just finished, open on his writing-table; Joseph had gone into the library and took the opportunity of my father's absence to add the postscript, exactly imitating his writing, and on his return my father duly folded the letter and sent it to the post without having perceived my brother's addition to it.

Another, not so harmless—but boys are mischievous—he played on an elderly woman, whom he met near Dublin when he was staying on a visit with some friends. He had never seen the woman before, and never saw her after; but she looked at him as if she recognized him, stopped and stood before him looking earnestly at his face, when the following dialogue ensued :—

Woman. "Oh, then, Masther Richard, is that yourself?"

Joseph. "Of course it is myself. Who else should I be?"

Woman. "Ah, then, Masther Richard, it's proud I am to see you. I hardly knew you at first, you're grown so much. Ah, but it's long since I seen any of the family. And how is the mistress and all the family?"

Joseph. "All quite well, thank you. But why don't you ever come to see us?"

Woman. "Ah, Masther Richard, don't you know I daren't face the house since that affair?"

Joseph. "Don't you know that is all forgotten and forgiven long ago? My mother and all would be delighted to see you."

Woman. "If I knew that, I'd have been up to the house long ago."

Joseph. "I'll tell you what to do—come up on Sunday to dinner with the servants. You know the hour; and you will be surprised at the welcome you will get."

Woman. "Well, please God, I will, Masther Richard. Good-bye, Masther Richard, and God bless you."

What sort of welcome the old lady (she had very probably been dismissed for stealing silver spoons) received on her arrival on the following Sunday has not transpired; but I dare say she was "surprised" at it.

One morning, about this time, our family prayers were interrupted in a comical way. A Captain and Mrs. Druid were staying with us for a few weeks. Having no child, their affections centred in a grey parrot, which they dearly loved, and on whose education most of their time was spent. And truly he was a wonderful bird. Amongst his other accomplishments, he sang "God save the King" in perfect tune; but he never could get beyond "happy and glorious." The last word seemed so to tickle his fancy, that he couldn't finish it, but went on singing "happy and glori-ori-ori-ori-ori-ori." He would also say, "Have you dined? Yes, sir. And on what? Roast beef, sir." Or, "As-tu déjeuné, mon petit Coco? Oui, monsieur. Et de quoi? Macaroni, monsieur."

For fear of accidents, he was not allowed into the breakfast-room till after prayers. One morning, however, by some mischance, he was there; but behaved with becoming decorum until prayers were nearly over. My father had got to the middle of the Lord's Prayer, when, in a loud voice, Poll called out, "As many as are of that opinion will say 'aye;' as many as are of the contrary opinion will say 'no.' The 'ayes' have it." I need hardly say, prayers were finished under difficulties.

This reminds me of a story which I heard, or read, not long since, of a gentleman who had a monkey and a parrot, to both of which he was much attached; but such was the enmity of the monkey to the parrot, that he never ventured to leave them by themselves. One morning he had just come down to breakfast, when he suddenly remembered that he had left them together in his bedroom. Upstairs he ran, three steps at a time, and into his room, where, to his horror, he saw the monkey, seated by the fire with a large heap of feathers before him. "Oh, you villain," he called out, "you have killed the parrot!" At the same moment he heard a slight rustling behind him, and, on turning round, saw the poor bird coming from under the bed with scarcely a feather except a few on his head, which he held on one side and said, "We've been having a devil of a time of it!"

CHAPTER II.

Lord Edward Fitzgerald's dagger—United Irishmen: the Apologia of John Sheares—Doctor Dobbin's kind deeds—The story of the Ilchester oak—An outlaw sportsman: his narrow escape and sad ending.

To return to my brother:—the tone of those early verses, from which I have given quotations, as well as that of some of his later ballads, was due to his mother, who, as a girl, had been in her heart more or less a rebel. She told him of the hard fate which, in '98, befell many of those whom she knew and admired. She told him much of Lord Edward Fitzgerald and the fight he made for his life, and showed him the dagger with which he fought for it. It is many years now since she gave me that dagger, and with it the following written account of how it came into her possession:—

"I was almost a child when I possessed myself of the dagger with which Lord Edward Fitzgerald had defended himself so desperately at the time of his arrest. The circumstances connected with it are these:—Mrs. Swan, wife of Major Swan (Deputy Town Major), was a relative of my mother. Our family constantly visited at her house in North Great George's

Street. My mother often took my younger sister and me there. I often heard Major Swan describe the dreadful struggle in which he had himself received a severe wound from the dagger which he had succeeded in wresting from Lord Edward, and which he took a pleasure in showing as a trophy. The dreadful conflict is described in the Annual Register, and in the journals of the day. The death-wound which Lord Edward received, and the death of Captain Ryan, are known to every one. The character of Lord Edward, the position which he held, and his tragical death, the domestic happiness which he had enjoyed, and the affection in which he held those near to him, I need not describe. When I saw the dagger in the hands with which Lord Edward had striven in the last fatal struggle for life or death, I felt that it was not rightfully his who held it, and wished it were in other hands. Wishes soon changed into plans, and I determined, if possible, to get it. I knew the spot in the front drawing-room where it was laid, and one evening, after tea, when Major Swan and his guests were engaged in conversation in the back drawing-room, I walked into the front drawing-room, to the spot where it was. I seized it and thrust it into my bosom, inside my stays. I returned to the company, where I had to sit for an hour, and then drove home a distance of three miles. As soon as we left the house I told my sister, who was beside me, what I had done. As soon as we got home, I rushed up to the room which my sister and I occupied, and, having secured the door, I opened one of the seams in the feather bed, took out the dagger, and plunged it among the feathers. For upwards of twelve years I lay every night upon the bed which contained my treasure. When I left home I took it with me, and it has been my companion in all the vicissitudes of life. When he missed it Major Swan was greatly incensed, and not without apprehensions that it had been taken to inflict a deadly revenge upon him. Had he taken harsh measures against the servants, whom he might have suspected, I had resolved to confess that I had taken it; but after a time his anger and uneasiness subsided. I have often seen and heard this dagger described as a most extraordinary weapon, and have been ready to laugh when I heard it so described. Moore mentions it in his life of Lord Edward Fitzgerald, as being in the possession of some other family. He is quite mistaken. This is the very dagger, which had not been many months in Major Swan's hands, when it became mine in the manner above described.

"EMMA L. LE FANU.

"April, 1847."

It will be seen from this what an enthusiastic admirer of Lord Edward my mother was. There were two other United Irishmen whom she knew well; they were the brothers Sheares, whose base and cruel betrayal by another United Irishman, who was their trusted friend and companion, caused such intense indignation amongst all who knew them. They were barristers and men of good position and means, sons of Henry Sheares, M.P., a banker in Cork, and were friends of my mother's father, the Rev. Doctor Dobbin. A short time before the capture of Lord Edward Fitzgerald they, with twelve other leaders of the insurrectionary movement, were arrested. The two brothers were tried for high treason and convicted, and were executed on the 14th of July, 1799. Amongst other letters of theirs I have two, which I give below, written, the one just before his sentence, the other the night before his execution, by John, the younger of the brothers. The first is to a Mr. Flemyng, a relative of my grandfather, the second to my grandfather himself.

"July 12, '98.

"DEAR HARRY,

"As I well know what will be my fate to-day, I enclose you a letter for my dear sister, which I request you will give her as soon after my execution as you shall think prudent. To such dear friends as you and William are, I know it is unnecessary to recommend my afflicted family, and particularly my ever-revered mother. I will require the performance of Doctor Dobbin's kind promise as soon as I feel myself fit to receive him. I did intend giving into your hands a short defence relative to some points in which I know I shall be vilely calumniated. But I have not had time, as I prepared every syllable of our defence, and wrote letters, etc., etc. One of you ought to be present at my execution, yet this is too much to ask. No, I must endure misrepresentation—the hearts of my friends will justify me. Farewell, my ever kind, my ever valued friends. I am called to court. Farewell for ever.

"Yours affectionately,
"JOHN SHEARES."

"To the Rev. Doctor Dobbin, D.D.
"Newgate, 12 o'clock at night,
"July 13th, 1798.

"MY DEAR SIR,

"As to-morrow is appointed for the execution of my brother and me, I shall trouble you with a few words on the subject of the writing produced on my trial, importing to be a proclamation. The first observation I have to make is that a considerable part of that scrolled production was suppressed on my trial, from what motive or whether by accident I will not say. Certain it is that the part which has not appeared must have in a great measure shown what the true motives were that caused that writing, if it had been produced. To avoid a posthumous calumny, in addition to the many and gross misrepresentations of my principles, moral and political, I shall state, with the most sacred regard to truth, what my chief objects were in writing, or rather in attempting to write it, for it is but a wretched patched and garbled attempt. It was contained in a sheet of paper, and in one or two pieces more which are not forthcoming.

"The sheet alone has been produced. It is written in very violent revolutionary language, because, as it in the outset imports, after a revolution had taken place could it alone be published. And the occurrence of such an event I thought every day more probable. The first sentence that has produced much misrepresentation is that which mentions that some of the most obnoxious members of Government have already paid the forfeit of their lives. I cannot state the words exactly. From this it is concluded that I countenanced assassination. Gracious God! but I shall simply answer that this sentence was merely supposititious, and founded on the common remark, oftenest made by those who least wished it verified, that if the people had ever recourse to force and succeeded, there were certain persons whom they would most probably destroy. The next most obnoxious sentence, more obnoxious to my feelings, because calculated to misrepresent the real sentiments of my soul, is that which recommends to give no quarter to those who fought against their native country, *unless they should speedily join the standard of freedom.** With this latter part of the sentence I found two faults, and therefore draw my pen over it as above. The first fault was that the word 'speedily' was too vague, and might encourage the sanguinary immediately to deny quarter, which is the very thing the sentence was intended to discountenance and prevent. The next fault was that it required more than ever should be required of any human being, namely, to fight against his opinions from fear. The sentence was intended to prevent the horrid measure of refusing quarter from being adopted by appearing to acquiesce in it at some future period, when the inhuman thirst for it should no longer exist. But as the sentence now stands, in two parts of the sheet, it would appear as if it sought to enforce the measure I most abhor. To prevent it was in fact one of my leading motives for writing the address. But I had also three others, that are expressed in the pieces of paper which made part of the writing, but which, though laid in the same desk, have disappeared. The three objects alluded to are these: the protection of property, preventing the indulgence of revenge, and the strict forbiddance of injuring any person for religious differences. I know it is said that I call on the people to take *vengeance* on their oppressors, and enumerate some of their oppressions; but this is the very thing that enables me to describe the difference between *private revenge* and *public vengeance*. The former has only a retrospective and malignant

---

* In the original a line is drawn with the pen through these words.

propensity, while the latter, though animated by a recollection of the past, has ever, and only, in view the removal of the evil and of its possibility of recurrence. Thus the assassin revenges himself, but the patriot avenges his country of its enemies by overthrowing them and depriving them of all power again to hurt it. In the struggle some of their lives may fall, but these are not the objects of his vengeance. In short, the Deity is said, in this sense, to be an *avenging* Being, but who deems Him *revengeful?*

"Adieu, my dear sir. Let me entreat you, whenever an opportunity shall occur, that you will justify my principles on these points.

"Believe me,
"Your sincere friend,
"JOHN SHEARES."

The Doctor Dobbin referred to in the first of these letters was my grandfather. He had been a Fellow of Trinity College, Dublin, but he resigned his fellowship in order to take to him a wife (the fellows had then to be celibate). The wife he took was Miss Catherine Coote, of Ash Hill Towers, in the county of Limerick, aunt of the late Sir Charles Coote. She died before I was born, but him I can remember well—a very small man in a full-bottomed wig, knee-breeches, black silk stockings, buckles in his shoes, and in his hand a gold-headed cane. He was long remembered in Dublin and its neighbourhood for his goodness and kindness to the poor, and many stories were told of his simplicity and charity. Once a man was begging at his carriage window; he had no change about him, so he handed the man a guinea, and said to him, "Go, my poor man, get me change of that, and I will give you a shilling."

I need hardly say he saw that beggar's face no more. Another day his wife, on coming home, found him in the hall with his hands behind his back. She soon perceived that he was hiding something from her, and insisted on knowing what it was. He timidly brought out from behind his back a leg of mutton which had been roasting in the kitchen, and which he had surreptitiously removed from the spit to give to a poor woman who was waiting at the door.

In our earlier days at Abington our favourite haunts for nutting and bird's-nesting were the Glen and the Old Deer Park of Cappercullen, which now form part of Glenstal, Sir Charles Barrington's picturesque demesne. In the Old Park there stood, and still stands, the Ilchester oak, one great bough of which stretched just to the edge of the drive, and there came nearly to the ground. Many a time we sat on this great bough, as many a boy and girl had done before, and by touching our feet to the ground, made it spring up and down; it was a perfect spring-board. I did not then know how the old tree had got its name, but many years afterwards I was told this story by my father-in-law, Sir Matthew Barrington :—

The Ilchester Oak.

'Tis well nigh a hundred years, perhaps more, since Cappercullen House was tenanted by a widower named O'Grady—not rich, but of an old and honoured family. He had one only daughter, Mary, the prettiest and merriest little maid in all that countryside, one of whose favourite sports was riding on this old oak bough. Prettier and prettier year by year the maiden grew, till, when just seventeen, at her first dance at a Limerick race ball, she was declared by all to be the loveliest and the brightest girl in the county, which was then, and I believe still is, famous for the beauty of its lasses. It was there she met young Lord Stavordale, eldest son of Lord Ilchester, who had just joined his regiment, and whose admiration she at once attracted. Afterwards they often met, for he lost no opportunity of seeing her as often as he could. He would ride out to Cappercullen, and join her in her walks with her father through the Glen and the Old Deer Park. Soon he loved her with all the ardour of first love. O'Grady saw that his daughter liked the bright and handsome young fellow, but knowing that Lord Ilchester would be sure to object to his eldest son marrying the daughter of a poor Irishman, and fearing that his daughter's affections should become too deeply engaged, he wrote to Lord Ilchester to the following effect:—" My Lord, I hope you will pardon the liberty I take in writing to you about your son. My only excuse is the great interest I take in the young man, and my fear that if he remains in Limerick he is likely to be involved in an unpleasant scrape. I would, therefore, most strongly advise you to have him moved elsewhere as soon as possible, and I trust to your honour that you will not tell him that I have written to you, or mention to him the subject of this letter." He received a reply full of gratitude, in which Lord Ilchester said that he regretted that he might probably never have an opportunity of thanking him in person for his kindness, but had requested his old friend, Colonel Prendergast, who was likely ere long to be in the south of Ireland, to call upon him to convey to him his thanks more fully than he could do by letter. Young Stavordale immediately disappeared from Limerick. The poor girl heard no more of him. She tried to be bright and cheery with her father, but he saw that her spirits sank, and that day by day she grew paler and more sad. Thus things went on for some months, when, late in autumn, a letter came from Colonel Prendergast to say that he expected to be in Limerick on the following Friday, and would, at Lord Ilchester's request, call to see Mr. O'Grady on Saturday, if he would receive him. O'Grady wrote to say he would be delighted to see him, and hoped he would be able to arrange to stay for some little time at Cappercullen. The Colonel arrived accordingly, and it was soon settled that he would stay for a week. At once he took a fancy to the girl, and many a walk they had together, and every day he was more charmed by her pale but lovely face, her gentle manners, and her pretty ways. The week was soon over, and the morning of his departure had arrived. Before leaving, he asked his host whether he could allow him to have a few words with him in private. When they were alone—

"I hope," he said, "you will forgive me for speaking to you about your daughter. I have been closely observing her, and, though you do not seem to see it, I greatly fear she is far from strong. I dread the winter here for her, and I venture to urge you strongly to take her to a warmer climate for a time."

"I am greatly obliged for the interest you take in my girl," said O'Grady; "but I am glad to say you are quite mistaken as to her health. I am convinced that there is nothing serious the matter with her, and trust she will very soon be as well as ever."

"I am afraid you are deceived," said the other. "She is so pale, and at times so depressed and sad, that I fear she is more seriously ill than you suppose."

"I see," said O'Grady. "I may as well tell you, in the strictest confidence, what is really the matter with her; but you must promise never to let Lord Ilchester know what I now tell you. It was about her that young Stavordale was making a fool of himself; it is about him that she is depressed, but as she has never heard of or from him since he left, she will very soon get over it."

Colonel Prendergast at once said, "My dear sir, you must really allow me to tell Lord Ilchester. I am certain if he knew what a charming girl, in every way, your daughter is, he would be only too glad that she should be his son's wife."

"No," said O'Grady; "you must never tell him. I know he would never consent to that."

"But I know he would," said the other, "for I am Lord Ilchester, and shall be proud to have such a wife for my son."

So they were wed, and many happy years they spent together. Long years have passed, and they are dead and gone; but the old Ilchester oak still stands in Cappercullen Park to remind us of them; and from this marriage are descended the present Earl of Ilchester and the Marquis of Lansdowne.

I give the story as it was told to me. I cannot vouch for the accuracy of all the details, but the main facts I believe to be perfectly true. Some years ago I told it to Miss Jephson, now Mrs. Boyle, and from it she took the plot of her charming novel, "An April Day."

Soon after we went to Abington there was, in our neighbourhood, a famous outlaw named Kirby, who was "on his keeping;" that is, in hiding from the police. He had been engaged in any number of agrarian outrages, amongst them the shooting of a landlord near Nenagh. The Government had offered a large reward for his capture, and the magistrates and police in the district were doing all in their power to take him. In his early days he had been passionately fond of races, hunts, and sports of every sort; and even now, when a price was set on his head, he could, sometimes, not resist the temptation of going to a hunt or coursing match. At some of these he narrowly escaped capture. Our friend and neighbour, Mr. Coote, who was a magistrate as well as a clergyman, on coming home from a coursing match, said to one of his men, "Who was that fine-looking fellow that was so active at the match?" "It's well for him," said the man, "that your honour didn't know him. That was Kirby."

Perhaps the narrowest escape Kirby had was one that also happened very near us. His mother, whom he rarely ventured to visit, lived in a one-roomed cottage about a mile from us, with her only other child, a daughter. One Sunday Kirby arrived, and, after much pressure from his mother, whom he had not seen for a long time, he consented to stay with her till the next day. Meantime an informer, hoping to secure the reward, went into Limerick and told Major Vokes that Kirby was almost certain to be at his mother's that night. Vokes held a position under Government analogous to that now held by a stipendiary magistrate. He was the most active magistrate in the south, and had detected more crime and brought more offenders to justice than any man in Ireland; and knowing how much it would add to his fame if he could arrest Kirby, he had often before searched the Widow Kirby's house for him, but never found any one there but herself and her daughter.

On this Sunday evening Kirby's sister, most

fortunately for the outlaw, had gone to a wake in the neighbourhood, and stayed out all night. The old woman had gone to bed, and Kirby was sitting by the fire, his pistols on the table beside him. For some years he had seldom spent a night in the house. When he did so, he sat, as he now was sitting, by the turf fire, where the slightest sound was sure to awake him. His mother had not long been in bed when he heard the sound of a horse and car approaching the house. He sprang to his feet and seizing the pistols, said to his mother—

"At any rate I'll have the life of one of them before I'm taken."

"Whisht, you fool!" said his mother. "Here, be quick! put on Mary's cap, take your pistols with you. Jump into bed, turn your face to the wall, and lave the rest to me."

He was scarcely in bed when there was a loud knocking at the door, which his mother, having lit a rush, opened as quickly as possible.

In came Major Vokes, accompanied by two constables, who had driven from Limerick with him. "Where is your son?" said Vokes.

"Plaze God, he's far enough from ye. It's welcome ye are this night," she said. "And thanks be to the Lord it wasn't yestherday ye came; for it's me and Mary there that strove to make him stop the night wid us; but thank God he was afeared."

They searched the house, but did not like to disturb the young girl in bed, and finding nothing, went, sadly disappointed, back to Limerick. The news of Kirby's escape soon spread through the country. Vokes was much chaffed, but Kirby never slept another night in his mother's house.

It was some months after this that the wife of a farmer who lived near Doon called one morning and asked to see our neighbour, Mr. Coote. When she came into his study, she said—

"Your reverence, could they do anything to Kirby if he was dead?"

"How could they, my good woman? What do you mean?"

"It's what I was afeared, your reverence, that they might send his body to the prison to be dissected by the doctors."

Mr. Coote, whom she thoroughly trusted, assured her that nothing of the kind could happen.

"Then," said she, "come with me and I'll show him to you dead."

He went to her house with her, and there he saw, lying dead on the bed, the fine young fellow whom he had, not long before, seen at the coursing match.

"When and how did he die?" he asked.

"Last night," they said, "he was stopping with us, and when he heard steps coming towards the house, thinking it might be the peelers, he ran out through the back-door, with his pistol in his hand, into the little wood. We heard a shot after he went, but we didn't much mind it at the time; but this morning we found him lying dead in the wood, with his foot caught in the briar that tripped him."

In his fall the pistol must have gone off. He was shot through the heart. I do not recollect a larger funeral than his.

CHAPTER III.

Faction fights: the Reaskawallahs and Coffeys — Paternal chastisement — A doctor in livery — I bear the Olive branch — Battles of the buryings — Dead men's shoes — Fairy Doctors: their patient spoils a coachman's toggery — Superstitions about birds.

WHEN we went to the county of Limerick there were many factions there—the Shanavests and Caravats, the Coffeys and the Reaskawallahs, the Three Years Old and Four Years Old. All these are now extinct except the last named, who still have a smouldering existence, in the neighbourhood of Emly, which occasionally flares up into a little blaze; but the glorious fights of other days are gone.

The factions nearest to us were the Coffeys and the Reaskawallahs, the latter so called from the name of a townland near Doon, where its chieftains had lived for generations. In our time its leader was John Ryan, generally called "Shawn Lucash" (*i.e.* John, the son of Luke), a powerful man who had led his men in many a hard-fought fight; while one Coffey of Newport was chief of the Coffeys.

The origin of their feud was, as in most other cases, lost in antiquity. The members of opposite factions, who happened to dwell near each other, lived peaceably together, except on the occasions when they met expressly for a fight. Fairs were the usual battlefields, though at times a special hour and place was fixed for a battle. I recollect one that was fought at Annagh Bog, near us, when the Coffeys were the victors; a few were killed and many on both sides dangerously wounded. The old story, often told, that the row began by one man taking off his coat and trailing it behind him, saying "Who will dare to tread on that?" is a myth. I have seen many a faction fight, every one of which began in the same way, which was thus: one man "wheeled," as they called it, for his party; that is, he marched up and down, flourishing his blackthorn, and shouting the battle-cry of his faction, "Here is Coffey aboo against Reaskawallahs; here is Coffey aboo— who dar strike a Coffey?"

"I dar," shouted one of the other party; "here's Reaskawallah aboo," at the same instant making a whack with his shillelagh at his opponent's head. In an instant hundreds of sticks were up, hundreds of heads were broken. In vain the parish priest and his curate ride through the crowd, striking right and left with their whips; in vain a few policemen try to quell the riot; on it goes till one or other of the factions is beaten and flies.

Just after one of these fights at the fair of

Abington, which I witnessed from the opposite bank of the river, I saw an elderly man running after a young fellow of two or three and twenty, every time he got near striking him on the head with a heavy blackthorn, and at every blow setting the blood streaming from his head. At last the youth got beyond his reach. "Why," said I to a man standing near me, "does that young fellow let the old man beat him in that savage way?" "Ah, sure, your honour," said he, "that's only his father that is chastising him for fighting."

The members of the Coffey faction were all men of that name, or their relatives and connections; the Reaskawallahs were nearly all Ryans, which is the most common name in that part of the county; so common that to distinguish one from another nearly every Ryan had a nickname, generally a patronymic, as Shawn Lucash, already mentioned. Another of the same faction was Denis Ryan, of Cuppanuke, always called "Donagh Shawn Heige" (Denis, son of John Timothy), his father being "Shawn Heige" (John the son of Timothy). There was also one Tom Ryan, whose son was Tom Tom, his son again Tommy Tom Tom, while Tommy Tom Tom's son was Tommy Tom Tom's Tommy. When not a patronymic the name had reference to some personal peculiarity, such as "Shamus na Cussa" (Jim of the Log), "Shawn Lauder" (Strong John), or "Leum a Rinka" (Bill of the dance).

In those days doctors and dispensaries were few

and far between, so the wounded generally came for treatment to our coachman, an amateur surgeon, who had been an officer's servant in the Peninsular War. His method was simple, somewhat painful, and supposed by the sufferers to be highly efficacious. He clipped the hair from about the wound, poured in turpentine mixed with whisky—this, of course, caused a yell—stitched the cut if a severe one, plastered it slightly, and then sent his patient home, equally amazed at his skill and charmed with his kindness.

Though, as I have said, we may still from time to time hear of a small faction fight in the south of Ireland, few men can remember them in their palmy days, where at every fair and market opposing factions met and many a head was broken. In 1829, towards the close of the agitation for Catholic emancipation, all this was changed. O'Connell and the priests, constantly speaking and preaching against England's hated plan of governing Ireland by *divide et impera*, unceasingly from platform and from altar urging the necessity of union, at last succeeded in reconciling the contending factions. Monster meetings and monster marchings, displays of physical forces, were organized. One of these great marchings, which passed close to our house, I saw, and indeed took part in it; for a friendly peasant induced me (it was nothing to me) to march some way in the procession carrying a green bough in my hand. It was the marching of the Reaskawallahs from their head-quarters near Doon to the headquarters of the Coffeys at Newport. They marched six deep, in military order, with music and banners, each man carrying, as an emblem of peace, a green bough; the procession was nearly two miles long. On its arrival at Newport the meeting was celebrated with much joy and whisky, and, in the presence of the priests, a treaty of perpetual peace was established, and never from that day did those factions meet again for battle. Similar reconciliations took place all over the country, and faction fighting practically ended. The peace established in other parts of Ireland did not, however, extend to the north, where the opposite parties were of a different sort—Orangemen v. Roman Catholics. They are now as ready for a fight as then, and are seldom long without one, and are expected to have a still livelier time if a Home Rule Bill should pass.

The fights which occasionally occurred at funerals, the so-called battles of the Derrins (buryings), had no connection with the regular faction fights, and continued long after the former had ceased. They never occurred except when there were two funerals on the same day, in the same churchyard, and not very often even then. They had their origin in the superstition that the last person buried in a churchyard has, in addition to his other troubles, to carry water to allay the thirst (in Purgatory) of all those previously buried there. His or her work

is incessant, day and night and in all weathers.
Where the water comes from I have never heard,
but as much is wanted, for the weather there is very
hot, the carrier of water is not relieved from his
arduous duties till another funeral takes place. So,
if there are to be two funerals at the same place
on the same day, the lively competition as to which
shall get first into the churchyard not unfrequently
leads to a fight. I have a vivid recollection of one
such fight in our neighbourhood, when much blood
flowed. It arose in this way. Two funerals were
approaching Abington Churchyard in opposite directions, one from Murroe, the other from Barrington's
Bridge. The former was nearing the churchyard
gate; on perceiving this the people in the other
funeral took a short cut by running across a field,
carrying the coffin with them, which they succeeded
in throwing over the wall of the churchyard before
the others were able to get in by the gate. This
was counted such sharp practice that they were at
once attacked by the other party, and a battle royal
ensued.

Peasants have been known to put shoes or boots
into coffins to save the feet of their relatives in
their long and weary water-carrying walks. Our
neighbour, John Ryan, of Cuppanuke, the Shawn
Heige whom I mentioned, put two pair of shoes in
the coffin of his wife—a strong pair for bad weather,
a light pair for ordinary wear.

Amongst many superstitions none was more

general than the belief that the fairies—"the good people," as the peasantry euphemistically call them—often take a child from its parents, substituting a fairy for it. This generally was supposed to happen when a child was very ill, especially if so ill as to be unable to speak. A chief part of the practice of fairy doctors, one or two of whom were sure to be found in every town, was to prescribe in cases of this kind. In the family of one of my father's labourers, Mick Tucker, such a case occurred. He and his wife Nell had an only child, Johnny, who at the time I speak of was about eight years old. He was very ill, and for some days had not spoken. One morning I went with my mother to their cottage to see how he was. To our surprise we found him lying on his bed, outside the bedclothes, his feet on the bolster, his head at the foot of the bed; on his chest a plate of salt, on which two rushes were placed across. On inquiry, we found that his mother had gone to Limerick the day before to consult Ned Gallagher, a fairy doctor of high repute in those days, and it was he who had prescribed this treatment, and had told her that under it the fairy would probably speak before evening, and declare what he wanted, and would depart. If, however, he did not, she was to light a turf fire opposite the house at twelve o'clock that night and hold the fairy over it on a shovel till he screamed, when he would at once vanish, the "good people" at the same moment restoring the stolen child.

This latter part of the prescription my father and mother determined to take steps to prevent; but there was no need to do so, for happily before night Johnny began to speak. He gradually recovered, but he, as well as his parents, ever after firmly believed that he had been away with the "good people," and he would tell strange stories of the wonderful places he had visited and the beautiful things he had seen when on his fairy rambles; while from his diminutive form and his wild ways many of the neighbours thought he was a fairy still. Some years afterwards he lived in the service of an aunt of mine in Dublin. He still often talked of his fairy life; he used to put out the light in the pantry and sit there in the dark alone, "pausing," as he called it. My aunt and cousins told me many a story of his strange behaviour.

I had myself an amusing adventure with him. I was on a visit with my aunt, and had to start for Limerick by the night mail coach. It happened to be the Queen's birthday, on which day the coachman and guards of the mail always got their new scarlet coats and gold lace hat-bands. All the coaches, too, were brightened up, and during the day went in procession through the streets, each drawn by four grey horses, the coachmen and guards resplendent in their new clothes and wearing large nosegays in their breasts. Precisely as the post-office clock struck eight on that and every evening, the mail coaches (there were eight or nine of them) followed each other from the post-office yard and passed into Sackville Street, where a crowd was always assembled to see the start. On that evening I had forgotten to take with me a parcel of ham-sandwiches which my aunt had ready for me. She found this out immediately after I had left her house, and told John Tucker to run after me with the parcel; but before he arrived the coach had started and was in Sackville Street. I was on the box-seat with the coachman, when I beheld John's figure emerging from the crowd, wildly shouting and gesticulating. He flung the package for me to catch; it missed me, but struck the coachman full on the chest. The parcel burst, and the beautiful new coat was spoiled with bread and ham, butter and mustard. The coachman used strong language, and gave John a good skelp with his whip, which made him scuttle off as fast as his little legs could carry him. I took no further notice, beyond saying to the coachman—

"What could that queer little fellow mean by flinging all that stuff at you?"

"Didn't you see, sir," said he, "that was a lunatic? Didn't you see the wild eyes of him, and the whole cut of him? Bad luck to him! he has destroyed my new coat."

As John grew older his eccentricities wore off, and for more than thirty years he was my faithful and trusted servant.

Amongst his other accomplishments, when a boy,

John was a very skilful bird-catcher, and an adept in making cribs and other traps; and many a thrush and blackbird he captured and ate, and many a robin he caught and let go. The robin (in Irish, the *spiddóge*) is, as is well known, a blessed bird, and no one, no matter how wild or cruel, would kill or hurt one, partly from love, partly from fear. They believe if they killed a robin a large lump would grow on the palm of their right hand, preventing them from working and from hurling. It is fear alone, however, that saves a swallow from injury, for it is equally well known that every swallow has in him three drops of the devil's blood. All other birds are fair game.

I was surprised last summer when in the county of Kerry to find a custom about robins still existing there, which I had thought was confined to the boys in Limerick and Tipperary. When a boy visited his crib, and in it, instead of the blackbird or thrush he hoped for, found a robin, his disappointment was naturally great. The robin he dare not kill, but he took the following proceedings. He brought the bird into the house, got a small bit of paper—printed paper was the best—put it into the robin's bill, and held it there, and addressed it thus: "Now, *spiddóge*, you must swear an oath on the book in your mouth that you will send a blackbird or a thrush into my crib for me; if you don't I will kill you the next time I catch you, and I now pull out your tail for a token, and that I may know you from any other robin." The tail was then pulled out, and the *spiddóge* let go—generally up the wide straight chimney. The boy well knew that he dare not carry out his threat, and when he caught a tailless robin, as there was nothing to pull out, he merely threatened him again and let him go. In very severe winters a robin with a tail was rarely to be seen.

CHAPTER IV.

Good will of the peasantry before 1831—A valentine—A justice's bulls—A curious sight indeed—Farms to grow fat on—Some cooks—" What the Dean wears on his legs "—Bloodthirsty gratitude—Old servants and their theories.

FROM the year 1826 to 1831 we lived on most friendly terms with the peasantry. They appeared to be devoted to us; if we had been away for a month or two, on our return they met us in numbers some way from our home, took the horses from the carriage and drew it to our house amid deafening cheers of welcome, and at night bonfires blazed on all the neighbouring hills. In all their troubles and difficulties the people came to my father for assistance. There was then no dispensary nor doctor near us, and many sick folk or their friends came daily to my mother for medicine and advice; I have often seen more than twenty with her of a morning. Our parish priest also was a special friend of ours, a constant visitor at our home. In the neighbouring parishes the same kindly relations existed between the priest and his flock and the Protestant clergyman. But in 1831 all this was suddenly and sadly changed when the tithe war, of which I shall say more by-and-by, came upon us.

Amongst our neighbours was a Mr. K——, who lived about five miles from us, and had a very pretty daughter, with whose beauty and brightness my brother, when about nineteen, was much taken. In those days it was the custom on St. Valentine's Day for every lover to send a " valentine " to the lady of his heart, so to Miss K—— he sent the following :—

> " Life were too long for me to bear
>   If banished from thy view;
> Life were too short a thousand year,
>   If life were passed with you.
>
> " Wise men have said, 'Man's lot on earth
>   Is grief and melancholy,'
> But where thou art there joyous mirth
>   Proves all their wisdom folly.
>
> " If fate withhold thy love from me,
>   All else in vain were given;
> Heaven were imperfect wanting thee,
>   And with thee earth were heaven."

After a few days he wrote to her the further lines which follow :—

> " My dear good madam,
>   You can't think how very sad I'm;
> I sent you, or mistake myself foully,
>   A very excellent imitation of the poet Cowley,
>   Containing three very fair stanzas,
> Which number, Longinus, a very critical man, says,
> And Aristotle, who was a critic ten times more caustic,

To a nicety fits a valentine or an acrostic.
And yet for all my pains to this moving epistle
I have got no answer, so I suppose I may go whistle.
Perhaps you'd have preferred that like an old monk I had
    pattered on
In the style and after the manner of the unfortunate
    Chatterton;
Or that, unlike my very reverend daddy's son,
I had attempted the classicalities of the dull, though
    immortal Addison.
I can't endure this silence another week;
What shall I do in order to make you speak?
   Shall I give you a trope
   In the manner of Pope,
  Or hammer my brains like an old smith
  To get out something like Goldsmith?
  Or shall I aspire on
  The same key touched by Byron,
  And laying my hand its wire on,
  With its music your soul set fire on
  By themes you ne'er can tire on?
   Or say,
   I pray,
   Would a lay
   Like Gay
  Be more in your way?
  I leave it to you,
  Which am I to do?
  It plain on the surface is
  That any metamorphosis,
  Which to effect you study,
  You may work on my soul or body.
Your frown or your smile makes me Savage or Gay
 In action, as well as in song;
And if 'tis decreed I at length become Gray,
 Express but the word, and I'm Young.
And if in the church I should ever aspire
 With friars and abbots to cope,
By a nod, if you please, you can make me a Prior—
 By a word you can render me Pope.

If you'd eat, I'm a Crabbe; if you'd cut, I'm your Steel,
  As sharp as you'd get from the cutler;
I'm your Cotton whene'er you're in want of a reel,
  And your livery carry, as Butler.
      I'll ever rest your debtor
     If you'll answer my first letter;
      Or must, alas! eternity
      Witness your taciturnity?
      Speak—and oh! speak quickly—
      Or else I shall grow sickly,
         And pine,
         And whine,
     And grow yellow and brown
      As e'er was mahogany,
      And lay me down
        And die in agony.
P.S. You'll allow I have the gift
    To write like the immortal Swift."

There were not many other gentry in our neighbourhood. One of those nearest to us was Captain Evans, of Ashroe, whose father had recently died. He had been a man of little education, but a stirring magistrate during the disturbances which had occurred some time previously. Many stories were told of him. It was said that in forwarding his reports on the state of the country to the authorities in Dublin Castle, he always began his letter, "My dear Government." In one of these reports he said, "You may rely on it, I shall endeavour to put down all nocturnal meetings, whether by day or by night." It was also told that in committing a man for climbing over his garden wall, he added the following words to the charge:—"He did there and then feloniously say that he would be damned if he wouldn't climb over it as often as he pleased." I forget whether it was he who was foreman of a jury in a libel case, in which the libel was that the plaintiff had been accused of stealing a goose. The verdict of the jury was, "We find for the plaintiff, with damages, the price of a goose."

Another neighbour of ours was the Rev. George Madder, Rector of Ballybrood, an old bachelor, who lived with a maiden sister, an elderly lady, solemn and stately, whom he held in great awe. She was very fond of flowers. When arranging some one morning in the drawing-room, she found a curious blossom which she had never seen before. Just as she discovered it her gardener passed the window, which was open. "Come in, James," she called to him; "I want to show you one of the most curious things you ever saw." James accordingly came in. Miss Madder sat down, not perceiving that the bottom of the chair had been lifted out. Down she went through the frame, nearly sitting on the floor. James went into fits of laughter, and said, "Well, ma'am, sure enough, it is one of the most curious things I ever seen in my life." "Stop, James," said she; "conduct yourself, and lift me out." "Oh, begorra, ma'am, I can't stop," said he; "it's so curious; it bates all I ever seen." It was some time before she could make him understand that her performance was not what he had been called in to see; and when he had helped her up, he was dismissed with a strong rebuke for his levity.

Mr. Madder was very fond of riding. He had bought a spirited young horse, which ran away with him and threw him; but he escaped with a few bruises. Shortly afterwards my father met him, and said, "I hope, Madder, you are none the worse for your fall." "I'm all right, thank you, Dean," said he. "And how is Miss Madder?" said my father; "she must have got a fright." "She is quite well," said he, "but rather skittish, rather skittish." He was rather deaf, and thought my father was inquiring for the mare, not for Miss Madder. I am not sure whether it was she who, when my father, at dinner, had helped her to turkey, at once said to him, "Sir, did you ever see a dean stuffed with chestnuts?" meaning of course to have asked, "Mr. Dean, did you ever see a turkey stuffed with chestnuts?"

Two of our more distant neighbours were Considine of Dirk and Croker of Ballinagard, both men of considerable property, and each having in his hands a large farm. It was a moot point which held the richer land; each maintained the superiority of his own. At one time Considine had a farm to let. A man from the county of Kerry, where the land is very poor, came to see it, with a view of becoming tenant. "My good man," said Considine, "I don't think you are the man to take a farm like this. It is not like your miserable Kerry land, where a mountain sheep can hardly get enough to eat. You don't know how the grass grows here!

It grows so fast and so high, that if you left a heifer out in that field there at night, you would scarcely find her in the morning." "Bedad, yer honour," replied the Kerry man, "there's many a part of my own county where, if you left a heifer out at night, the devil a bit of her you'd ever see again!"

In a dispute as to the comparative merits of their farms, "I tell you what," said Considine, "an acre of Dirk would fatten a bullock." "Don't tell me!" said Croker; "an acre of Ballingard would fatten a bullock and a sheep." "What is that to Dirk?" said the other; "I tell you an acre of Dirk would fatten Spaight of Limerick." Spaight was a merchant in Limerick, the thinnest man in the county.

This reminds me of a story recently told me of a Roman Catholic bishop, one of the most agreeable men in Ireland. Cardinal Manning, who was, as we all know, as thin and emaciated as "Spaight of Limerick," when in Liverpool was visiting a convent where an Irishwoman was cook. She begged and prayed for the blessing of the cardinal. The lady superior presented the request to him, with which he kindly complied. The cook was brought in, knelt down before him, and received his blessing; whereupon she looked up at him, and said, "May the Lord preserve your Eminence, and oh, may God forgive your cook!"

Apropos of cooks, I may here mention one who lived with my grandmother, and had formerly been cook to a Mrs. Molloy, a lady who was housekeeper to the Irish House of Lords, and who had recently died. The cook never ceased talking of Mrs. Molloy, holding her up to the fellow-servants as the highest authority on all points, saying, "Mrs. Molloy wouldn't have done this," or "Mrs. Molloy wouldn't have allowed that." This irritated the servants, and one day, as she was holding forth in this way, the butler said to her, "For God's sake, let the woman rest in her grave!" She drew herself up with much dignity, and said, "Mrs. Molloy was no woman; she was a lady; and I'll not let her rest in her grave for you or for any man." She described Mrs. Molloy's splendour when going to the castle, "with a turbot on her head, with beautiful oxe's feathers in it." It was she who, hearing her mistress tell the kitchen-maid to say "peas," not "pays," said to her, "Don't mind her; say 'pays,' as your honest mother and father did before you."

Another neighbour of ours was a retired barrister, named Holland, a pompous old gentleman, who lived at Ballyvoreen, about two miles from us.

One Saturday afternoon two of my father's gaiters, both for the same leg, had been sent for repair to one Halloran, a shoemaker in the village of Murroe, not far off, with strict orders to him to mend one, at least, of them that evening, and send it home early next morning. It was near eleven o'clock on Sunday morning—service began at twelve—and the gaiters had not arrived, so the servant told the stable-boy, a wild-looking youth, and as wild as he looked, to run off as fast as he could to Halloran's, and to bring the gaiters, done or undone—not to come without them. "What is a gaiter?" said the boy. "What the Dean wears on his legs," said the servant. The boy thought the man had said Holland's, not Halloran's, and so off he ran to Ballyvoreen, rang violently at the hall door, and, when a servant appeared, said, "Give me what the Dane wears on his legs." "What do you mean?" said the servant. "I mane what I say, and I must get it, done or undone, so you may as well give it to me at once." Mr. Holland, hearing loud voices in the hall, came out and asked what the noise was about. "Give me," said the boy, "what the Dane wears on his legs." "The boy is mad," said Holland. "I'm not mad. I must have it, done or undone, and I wonder at a gentleman of your affluence refusing to give it up; but it's no use for you, for I won't go till I get it." Supposing him to be a lunatic, Holland shut the door, and the boy had finally to go home. Meantime Halloran had sent the gaiters in time for my father to wear them going to church.

Some years after this the same boy acted as my fishing attendant or gillie, and, later on, when I was in Dublin, wrote to me to say that he was anxious to emigrate to America, and begging that I would send him a little money to help him to do so. I sent him a few pounds, and received from him the following letter:—

"Honoured Sir,
"God bless you for what you sent me. If I gets on I'll send as much back; but if I dies, plaze God I'll meet you in the Lizzum fields, and pay your honour then. But any way you always have the prayers of your humble servant,
"Michael Brien.
"P.S.—Is there any one here that ever done anything to injure or offend you, that your honour would like anything to be done to? I'd like to do something for your honour before I goes, to show how thankful I am."

When speaking of our coachman, the amateur surgeon, I forgot to mention that he loved to bring in a few French words, which he had picked up in his travels. One day as he drove across a ford on the Bilboa river, near Doon, seeing that my mother was rather frightened, he turned to her and said, "Never fear, madam; but, indeed, if you had a *faux pas* of a coachman instead of me you might be drowned." Another day he had been telling me of a robbery of a large quantity of plate from Mr. Loyd's house at Tower Hill. "I wonder," I said to him, "how they disposed of all that plate." "You may be sure," he said, "they sent it up to them connoisseurs in Dublin."

My father's sexton was named Young—a queer old fellow too. When asked his name by any one, his invariable reply was, "Well, sir, I'm Young by name, but old by nature." One Sunday morning in the vestry room my father could not find his stole. "This is most provoking," said he; "the congregation will wonder why I do not wear it to-day." "Let them wonder," said Young; "but what does it signify if your raverence had not a tack upon you, so long as you preach a good sermon?"

Another day one of the parishioners having died very suddenly, my father said to him, "How terribly sudden the death of poor Keys was!" "Ah! your raverence," said he, "the Lord gave that poor man no sort of fair play."

In ploughing a field near the rectory, some old coins had been found; when Young saw some of them he said he did not think they could be very old, for "Don't you see the family of the Rexes was on the throne when they were made?"

The same mistake has been made by others. Darwin mentions that when in Chili he found a Cornish man, who was settled there, who thought that "Rex" was the name of the reigning family.

My nurse, who still lived with us, said she was sure the coins must have been hid there by the bishops. "What bishops?" I asked her. "The bishops that conquered Ireland long ago," said she. On my telling her that bishops had never conquered this country, "Well," said she, "it must have been the danes (deans), or clergy of some sort."

When first we were at Abington, a peasant girl came two or three times to the rectory with a hare and other game for sale. My father wishing to ascertain whether she came by them honestly, asked her where she got them. "Sure, your raverence," said she, "my father is poacher to Lord Clare."

Something of the same sort occurred five and

twenty years later. When I was engaged as engineer on the railway from Mallow to Fermoy, then in course of construction, a friend asked me to get employment for a man who lived near Doneraile, in whom he felt an interest. I succeeded in getting him a good post under the contractor; he wrote me a letter full of gratitude. He had no doubt heard that I was fond of fishing, and must have thought that what I liked best was eating the trout, not catching them, for to his letter was added the following postscript: " I understand your honour is fond of trouts, so I hopes before long to send your honour some good ones, for I do, sometimes, draw my Lord Doneraile's preserves by night." Lord Doneraile very strictly preserved his part of the Awbey river (Spencer's " gentle Mullagh "), which is famous for the size and beauty of its trout.

It was in the year 1838 that Father Mathew, one of the simplest minded men I have ever known, began his noble temperance work, which soon was crowned with such marvellous and unparalleled success. I have seen several of his monster meetings, where thousands took the pledge; many of the great processions too, marching to meetings. As one of these with bands and banners passed through Sackville Street, a tipsy man, leaning with his back to the railings, was gazing at it with a contemptuous stare, and as my brother and I passed by him we heard him say, " What are they after all ? what are they but a pack of cast drunkards ? "

Another drunken man, whom a friend was trying to bring to his home some miles away, was constantly crossing from one side of the road to the other, so his friend said to him, "Come on, Pat, come on; the road is long." "I know it is long," said Pat; "but it isn't the length of it, but the breadth of it that is killing me."

It was only a few months ago that I was told of a man, in like condition, who was knocked down by the buffer of an engine, which was shunting some waggons, near Bray station. He was stunned for a moment, but very slightly hurt. The porters ran to his assistance. One of them said, "Bring him to the station at once." He thought they meant the police station. "What do you want to take me to the station for?" said he. "You know who I am; and if I have done any damage to your d—— machine, sure I'm able to pay for it?"

CHAPTER V.

The tithe war of 1831 : the troops come to our village—A marked man—" Push on ; they are going to kill ye ! "—Not his brother's keeper—Boycotting in the thirties—None so dead as he looked—Lord Cloncurry's manifesto—A fulfilled prophecy.

IN 1831 came the tithe war, and with it our friendly relations with the priests and people ceased. The former, not unnaturally, threw themselves heart and soul into the agitation. The Protestant clergy were denounced by agitators and priests from platform and from altar, and branded as the worst enemies of the people, who were told to hunt them like mad dogs from the country; they were insulted whereever they went, many were attacked, some were murdered. It is hard now to realize the suddenness with which kindness and good-will were changed to insult and hate; for a short time we were not so badly treated as some of the neighbouring clergy, but the people would not speak to us, and scowled at us as we passed.

Of Doon, a parish which adjoined Abington, our cousin, the Rev. Charles Coote, was rector. At the very commencement of the agitation he had given much offence by taking active measures to enforce the payment of his tithes. It was thus his fight began. He had for years been on the most intimate and friendly terms with Father H——, the parish priest, who held a considerable farm, for which Mr. Coote would never allow him to pay tithe. When the agitation against tithes began, Father H—— preached a fierce sermon against them, denouncing Mr. Coote from the altar, telling the people that any man who paid one farthing of that "blood-stained impost" was a traitor to his country and his God. "Take example by me, boys," he said; "I'd let my last cow be seized and sold before I'd pay a farthing to that scoundrel Coote." On hearing of this, Mr. Coote wrote to ask him whether the report he had heard was true; he replied that he was proud to say that it was true, adding, "You may seize and sell my cattle if you can, but I'd like to see the man that would buy them." Coote, who was a brave and determined man, was so indignant that he resolved to fight it out with the priest. He gave orders to his bailiff, and next morning at break of day, before any one dreamt that he would make the attempt, one of the priest's cows was taken and impounded. Public notice was given that, on a day and hour named, the cow would be sold in Doon; counter notices were posted through the country telling the people to assemble in their thousands to see Father H——'s cow sold. Mr.

Coote went to Dublin to consult the authorities at the Castle, and returned next day, with a promise from the Government that they would support him.

Early on the morning fixed for the sale I was sitting at an open window in our breakfast-room, when my attention was roused by the sound of bagpipes playing " The Campbells are Coming." On looking in the direction whence the sound came, I saw four companies of Highlanders, headed by their pipers, marching down the road, followed by a troop of lancers and artillery with two guns.

On this little army went to Doon, where many thousands of the country people were assembled. At the appointed hour the cow was put up for sale. There was a belief then prevalent among the people that at a sale unless there were at least three bidders, nothing could be sold; under this mistaken idea, a friend of the priest bid a sum, much beyond her value, for the cow; she was knocked down to him, he was obliged to hand the money to the auctioneer, and the tithe was paid. During all this time, except shouting, hooting at the soldiers, and " groans for Coote," nothing was done; but when the main body of the troops had left the village shots were fired, and volleys of stones were thrown at four of the lancers who had remained after the others as a rear guard. They fired their pistols at their assailants, one of whom was wounded. The rest of the lancers, hearing the shots, galloped back and quickly dispersed the crowd. It was weary work for the troops, as the day was very hot and bright, and their march to and from Doon was a long one, that village being certainly not less than fifteen miles from Limerick. On their return they bivouacked and dined in a field close to us, surrounded by crowds of the peasantry, many of whom had never seen a soldier before; after a brief rest the pipes struck up, " The Campbells are Coming," and they were on their march again. So ended this, to us, memorable day.

The next morning, as we were at breakfast, the room door opened; an old man came in; he fell on his knees and cried, " Oh, wirasthru, my little boy is killed, my boy is shot! Sure the craythur was doin' nothing out of the way when the sogers shot him. Oh, Vo! Vo! What will I ever do widout my little boy!" "What can I do for you, my poor man?" said my father. "Ah! then it's what I want your honour to give me a bit of note that'll get him into the hospital in Limerick."

My father at once gave him the order for his son's admission. He departed invoking blessings on us, and shedding tears of gratitude.

As we afterwards found, the "little boy" was a youth of six and twenty, who had got a slight flesh wound in the leg. They never brought him to the hospital, but they paraded him, all day, through the streets of Limerick, lying in a cart, covered with a blood-stained sheet; to the back of the cart a board was fixed, on which, in large letters, was this inscription, "THESE ARE THE BLESSINGS OF TITHES." From that day Mr. Coote was a marked man.

Wherever he or any of his family were seen they were received with shouts and yells, and cries of "Mad dog! mad dog! To hell with the tithes! Down with the tithes!" One afternoon, when we returned from a visit to the rectory at Doon, we received a message from our parish priest to say that if we went there any more we should be treated as the Cootes were. Accordingly on our return from our next visit to them, shouts and curses followed us all the way home; from that day forward, when any of us (or even our carriage or car) was seen, the same shouts and cursing were heard in all directions. On one occasion this gave rise to an incident which amused us much. Anster, a poet popular in Dublin, and well known there as the translator of Goethe's "Faust," and author of many pretty poems, came to spend a few days with us. As he drove from Limerick on our car, the usual shouting followed him; being slightly deaf, he heard the shouts only, not the words of threatening and abuse. At dinner, with a beaming countenance, he said to my father, "Mr. Dean, I never knew I was so well known down here, but one's fame sometimes travels further than we think. I assure you, nearly the whole way as I drove from Limerick I was loudly cheered by the people." When we told him what the cheering was, the form of his visage changed.

At this time none of us went out alone, and we were always well armed. This the people knew, and did not actually attack any of us except on two occasions. On one of these my sister, who till a few months before had been idolized by the people for her goodness to them and untiring work amongst them, thought that if she and two girls, cousins, who were with us at the time, drove out by themselves, they would not be molested, especially as she had recently been in very delicate health. So taking advantage of an hour when the rest of the family were out, they went for a drive, when not only were they received with the usual hooting, but were pelted with mud and stone. One of the girls had a front tooth broken and they were glad to get home without further injury, and never again ventured to go out without protection.

The other attack happened thus. My father had been persuaded by some friends to try whether offering a large abatement, and giving time, might induce some of the farmers to pay at least some part of the tithes then due. A number of circulars offering such terms were prepared. These my cousin, Robert Flemyng, and I (little more than boys at the time) undertook to distribute, and to explain the terms to the farmers whose houses we proposed to visit. On our first day's ride nothing worth mentioning beyond the usual hooting occurred. Some of the houses were shut against us as the inmates saw us approach; at some few we were not uncivilly received, but were distinctly told that under no circumstances would one farthing of tithes ever be paid again.

On the following day we rode to a different part of the parish, to visit some farmers in the direction of Limerick. As we turned off the main road down a by-road leading to the village of Kishiquirk, we saw a man standing on a hillock holding in his hands a spade, high in air, then lowering the spade and giving a shrill whistle, then holding up the spade again. We knew this must be a signal, but for what we couldn't think. When we reached the village, a considerable and very threatening crowd was collected there, who saluted us with "Down with the Orangemen! Down with the tithes!" As this looked like mischief, we drew our pistols from our pockets, and each holding one in his right hand, we rode slowly through the throng. As we got near the end of the village a woman called to us, " What are ye riding so slow for ? Push on, I tell you ; they are going to kill ye!" We did push on, and with some difficulty, by riding one after the other, got past a cart which was hastily drawn across the road to stop us. On we galloped, showers of stones after us as we went. About a quarter of a mile further on another but smaller crowd awaited us ; they were not on the road, but just inside the mound fence which bordered it. On this mound they had made ready a good supply of stones for our reception, but, seeing us hold our pistols towards them, they did not venture to throw the stones till just as we had passed them, when they came after us volley after volley. Many a blow we and our horses got, but none that stunned. One man only was on the road, and, as we got near him, I saw him settling his spade in his hand as if to be ready to strike a blow. I presented my pistol at him. " Don't shoot me," he called out; " I'm only working here." But just as I passed him he made a tremendous blow at me; it missed me, but struck the horse just behind the saddle. The spade was broken by the violence of the blow. Down went the horse on his haunches, but was quickly up again, and on we went. Had he fallen, I should not have been alive many minutes; he brought me bravely home, but never recovered, and died soon afterwards.

As we neared our house we met a funeral, headed by the Roman Catholic curate of the parish. We rode up to him, covered as we and our horses were with mud and blood, in the vain hope that he would say some words of exhortation to the people. " See," we said, " Father M——, how we have been treated when we were on a peaceful and friendly mission to some of your flock." " I suppose," said he, " ye were unwelcome visitors." " Is that any reason," said I, " that they should try to murder us?" " It's no business of mine," said he, and passed on.

A proclamation, as fruitless as such proclamations then were, and now are, was issued by the Government offering a reward to any one who would give such information as would lead to the conviction of any of the men who had attacked us. It was well we had not gone that day to visit a farmer in another direction, where, as we afterwards learned, four armed men lay in wait, in a plantation by the road, to shoot us.

Mr. Coote was much surprised when he heard all this. He had always said, "Let them shout and hoot as they will, in their hearts they like us too well to shoot either you or me, or any one belonging to us." A few weeks later he was painfully undeceived. As he rode home from church he stopped his horse, as he had often done before, to let him take a mouthful of water from a little stream which crossed the road; he had scarcely stopped when a thundering report, which nearly deafened him, and a cloud of smoke came from a little grove close beside him. The blunderbuss which had been aimed at him had burst: its shattered remains, a half-emptied bottle of whisky, and a quantity of blood were found in the grove. Hearing of this, I went next day to see him. Never did I see a man more saddened and disappointed. He said, "I would not have believed it would ever come to this."

Boycotting, supposed to be a recent invention (in reality only new in name), was put in force against the clergy, to whom the people were forbidden to speak. Placards were posted all through the neighbourhood ordering that no one should work for Mr. Coote on pain of death.

There lived near Doon six stalwart young fellows, brothers, named Lysaght, whom some years previously Mr. Coote, being fully convinced of their innocence, had by his exertions saved from transportation, to which, on perjured evidence, they had been sentenced. The real culprits were afterwards arrested and convicted. These six fellows were determined to work for their benefactor, so they, with some Protestant parishioners of his, assembled one fine morning on the bog of Doon, to cut his turf. Suddenly about midday crowds of men appeared crossing the bog from all sides towards the workmen, shouting and firing shots. The turf-cutters ran for their lives to the rectory, not waiting to put on their coats. The mob came on, tore up the clothes, destroyed the turf that had been cut, smashed the turf-cutting implements, and then retired as they came, with shouts and shots.

We were not "boycotted" to the same extent, and were allowed to cut our turf and save our crops. One morning we heard a rumour that our labourers, who were saving our hay, were to be stopped, and we were preparing for an attack, when our steward said, "You needn't be a morsel uneasy, for it would be *illegal* for them to come to annoy us without giving us regular proper notice."

The Lysaghts, whom I have mentioned as helping Mr. Coote in his difficulties, were amongst the coolest and most determined fellows I ever met. They had been among the bravest of the Reaskawallahs, and by their prowess had often turned the tide of war, and won the victory in their battles with the Coffeys.

One evening, just as Mr. Coote had got off his horse at his hall door, a man ran up to him, and said, " Oh, your honour, they are murdering Ned Lysaght there below on the road to Cappamore."

He remounted his horse at once, and galloped down the road, where he found Lysaght lying in a pool of blood, apparently dead, and saw three men running away across the fields. He jumped off his horse, knelt down beside Ned, and said, " Ah, my poor dear fellow, have they killed you ? "

Ned opened his eyes, and sat up, blood streaming from his head and face. " Thanks be to the Lord, I'm not killed entirely ; but they thought I was. They kem up, unknownst to me, behind me, and one of them struck me wid a stone, and tumbled me. As soon as I was down the three of them bate me wid sticks and stones till they thought I was dead. I didn't purtind to be dead too soon, in dread they'd know I was scaming ; but when one of them gev me a thremendious crack on the head, I turned up my eyes, and ' Och, dhe alamon am ' (' God, take my soul '), says I, and shtiffend my legs and my arms, and, begorra, they were full sure it's what I was dead ; and, till I heard your honour's voice, I never opened an eye, or stirred hand or fut, in dhread they might be watchin' me."

" Do you know them ? " asked Mr. Coote.

" I partly guess who one of them was ; but I

F

couldn't be too sure, for they all had their faces blackened," said he.

After a few minutes Lysaght was able, with Mr. Coote's help, to walk back to the rectory, and in a few weeks he was as well and strong as ever.

During the tithe war the following characteristic circular was sent by Lord Cloncurry to the tenants on his large property in my father's parish. The Mr. Robert Cassidy mentioned was his agent, who took an active part in the agitation against tithes.

<p style="text-align:center">" TITHES.
" <i>Lord Cloncurry to his Tenants.</i></p>

"I am told that Mr. Robert Cassidy has advised you not to pay tithes. I hope it is not so, for I never authorized him so to do. If tithe was abolished to-morrow, all new leases would be at an increased rent. The poor man would then be far worse off than under the composition, which makes tithe comparatively light to the small holder and potatoe-grower.

"I think Parliament will soon make a different provision for Protestant clergy, and not call on the Roman Catholics to pay them; but I hope the landlords will pay tithe for the support of the poor and other useful purposes; and, until the law be changed, I think all honest and wise men should obey it, even in its present offensive and, I must add, unjust state.

"Your affectionate friend and landlord,
"CLONCURRY."

It is a remarkable fact that his grandson, the present Lord Cloncurry, was the first landlord in Ireland to make a bold, and so far successful, defence of his rights against the "No Rent" agitation of the Land League on this very same property.

During all these troublous times the landlords

looked on with indifference, and showed little sympathy with the clergy in their difficulties. My brother used to say, "Never mind, their time will come; rents will be attacked, as tithes are now, with the same machinery, and with like success." His prophecy was laughed at. Long after, one who had heard him said to him, "Well, Le Fanu, your rent war hasn't come." All he said was, "'Twill come, and soon too." And, as we know, come it did with a vengeance.

In 1832 Lord Stanley (afterwards Lord Derby), then Chief Secretary for Ireland, who was a friend of my father's, placed him on a commission, appointed by the Government to make inquiries and investigations respecting tithes with a view to legislation. This necessitated his residence in or near Dublin for a considerable time, so we left Abington and all our troubles there, and did not return till nearly three years later. Meantime, the tithe question having been settled by Parliament, the country had settled down into its normal state; and though the old cordial relations with the peasantry never could be quite restored, still, we lived on friendly terms with them till my father's death in 1845.

CHAPTER VI.

The pleasures of coaching—I enter at Trinity College, Dublin—A miser Fellow: Anecdotes about—Whately, Archbishop of Dublin, and his legs—The vocative of cat—Charles Lever's retort-courteous to the Bishop.

TRAVELLING in those days—sixty years ago—was an affair very different from what it now is. The journey from Limerick to Dublin, a distance of a hundred and twenty miles, was a serious undertaking. If you wanted a seat inside the coach, you had to secure it three or four days beforehand; if outside, a day or two before the day on which you meant to travel. The day coach, which carried seventeen passengers, four inside and thirteen out, nominally performed the journey in fourteen hours, but practically took two hours more. The night mail, which was very punctual, did it in twelve hours; it carried only eight passengers, four outside and four in. Of the outside travellers, one sat on the box beside the coachman, and three on the seat behind him. The back of the coach was occupied by the mail-bags and the guard, or guards (there were sometimes two), who were armed with brass-barrelled blunderbusses and pistols to guard the mails, as the mail-coaches were occasionally attacked and robbed. The coach was comparatively small, and, with people of any size, it was a tight fit to squeeze four into it. As soon as the four unhappy passengers were seated, and had put on their night-caps, the first thing was to arrange their legs so as to incommode each other as little as possible; the next was to settle which of the windows was to be open, and how much of it. This was seldom settled without a good deal of bickering and dispute. The box-seat, which was the favourite in the day coach, was least sought for in the mail; and rightly so, for it was hard to keep awake all night, and if you fell asleep, you couldn't lean back—there was nothing to lean on; the box-seat had no back. If you leant to the right, you fell against the coachman, who awoke you with a shove, and requested you would not do that again; if you did it again, he gave you a harder shove, and used some strong language. If you leant to your left, you did it at your peril; the low rail at the side of the seat could not prevent your falling off; it was only about four inches high. How often have I wakened with a start, when I was all but over, resolved to sleep no more. Vain resolution! In ten minutes I was fast asleep again, again to be awakened with another frightful start; and so on for the greater part of the night. A few years later, when I had constantly to travel by night, I adopted the device of strapping myself to the seat with a strong leather strap.

Besides the two I have mentioned, there was a third, the Birr coach, so called because it broke the journey at the town of Birr, now called Parsonstown from the family name of Lord Rosse, whose fine demesne and castle adjoin the town. This coach took two days to perform the journey, and was on that account much patronized by ladies, children, and invalids, for whom the long day's journey in the day coach was too fatiguing. It was a fine roomy vehicle, carrying six inside.

It was by this coach that most of our party made our journey from Abington to Dublin. My father, with my brother, had started a day or two before the rest of the family, to have things ready for us in Dublin. We followed—my mother, my sister, a cousin who had been staying with us, and myself—inside the coach, with a lady and gentleman whom we did not know. On the outside were my mother's maid, a man-servant, fifteen other passengers, and a huge pile of luggage on the roof. We got to Birr in time for supper, and had to be up at five next morning, as the coach was to resume its journey at six. It was pitchy dark and snowing thickly when we started. About four miles from Birr the road passes through a bog. As there was about seven inches of snow on the ground, it was not easy for the coachman to see the edge of the road distinctly. He went too much to one side, the off wheels went into a hollow, and in an instant over went the coach on its side. The outside passengers were flung into the bog, but were saved from injury by the softness of the snow and turf—none of them were hurt; while we inside had our hands and faces cut by the broken glass of the windows.

After walking a mile we reached a cabin, whose inmates entertained us till the coach was put upon its legs again, fresh harness brought from Birr, and the luggage repacked. It was nearly four hours before we were on the road again, and we arrived five hours behind our time in Dublin. This kind of mishap was not uncommon in the good old coaching days.

During our residence in Dublin, my brother and I entered Trinity College, where we subsequently took our degrees; but our names being on the country list, we were enabled for the greater part of the year to live at Abington, only coming up periodically to the examinations in the University.

Some years previously one of the Fellows, Doctor Barrett, better known as Jackey Barrett, a remarkable character, had died. He had been equally famous as a miser and a Hebrew scholar. Of him many a story was told, well known then to the students. Many of them are now forgotten, and some at least will, I hope, be new to my readers. He had never, it was said, but once been out of

Dublin, rarely outside the College gates. He dined at Commons; his only other meal was his breakfast, consisting of a penny loaf and a halfpennyworth of milk. Every morning he handed a halfpenny to the old woman who looked after his rooms, and sent her out to buy the milk. One frosty morning she slipped, fell, and broke her leg. She was taken to a hospital, and for once Barrett ventured beyond the College precincts, and went to see her. "Well, Mary," he said to her, "do you see me now, I suppose the jug is broken, but where is the halfpenny?"

As a rule he prefaced everything he said with the words, "Do you see me now." Having never been in the country, he had scarcely seen a bird, except the sparrows which hopped about the College courts. The only time he was known to have been out of Dublin was when he had been summoned to Naas, in the county of Kildare, to give evidence in some law case. As he stood in the stable-yard of the inn he saw a cock on the opposite side of the yard, and addressed the ostler thus—

"My good man, do you see me now, what is that beautiful bird over there?"

Ostler. "Ah, go away with you! You know what it is as well as I do."

Barrett. "Indeed I do not; and I'll be greatly obliged if you'll tell me."

Ostler. "Ah, get out; you're a-humbugging me! You know well enough it's a cock."

Barrett. "Is it, indeed? I thank you exceedingly."

After his death, in the margin of the page in Buffon's "Natural History," where the cock is described, there was found in Barrett's hand these words: "The ostler was right; it *was* a cock."

At a discussion at the College Board as to how to get rid of a huge heap of rubbish which lay in the College Park, Barrett suggested that they should dig a hole and bury it.

"But, Doctor Barrett," said they, "what shall we do with the stuff that comes out of the hole?"

"Do you see me now," said he; "dig another and bury it."

One morning when a company of the College corps (volunteers) were being drilled in the College Park, Barrett happened to pass by. To show respect to him, as a Fellow of College, the officer in command gave the word "Present arms!" when to his surprise he saw Barrett tucking up his gown and running away as fast as his legs would carry him. Barrett, on being asked afterwards why he ran away, said, "Well, do you see me now, I heard the officer saying 'Present!' and I knew the next word would be 'Fire!' and if I didn't run I'd have been shot."

At this time he was a great friend of a brother Fellow, Magee, afterwards Bishop of Raphoe, and finally Archbishop of Dublin, who was grandfather of the late Archbishop of York, and was the only person to whom Barrett ever lent money. He wanted a loan of five pounds, and went to see Barrett in his rooms, who agreed to make the loan, went into his bedroom, and returned with an old stocking full of guineas in his hand. Just as he came into the room the stocking burst, and the guineas were scattered on the floor. Magee stooped down to help Barrett to pick them up.

"Stop, stop, Magee!" said he. "Do you see me now, get up and stand on that table, and I'll pick them up."

The loan was then made, and Magee left him counting the guineas.

A few days afterwards he met him, and said, "I hope, Barrett, you found your guineas all right?"

"Well, do you see me now," said Barrett, "they were all right but one. One was gone; and maybe it rolled into a mouse-hole, Magee, and *maybe it didn't.*"

He afterwards quarrelled with Magee, and, detesting him as much as he had liked him, could not bear to hear his name mentioned. When Magee was made bishop, the other Fellows used to tease Barrett by asking him whether he had heard of Magee's promotion. On one such occasion he replied—

"No, I haven't heard of it, and moreover I don't want to hear of it."

"Didn't you hear," said they, "he has been made Bishop of Raphoe?"

"Do you see me now," said Barrett, "I don't care if he was made bishop of hell so long as I am not in his lordship's diocese."

Barrett was Professor of Hebrew. He was examining a class in the Psalms. One of the students, not knowing his work at all, was prompted by one Dickinson, a good Hebrew scholar, who sat next him, and said aloud—

"And the hills skipped like rams."

"Yes," said Barrett, "do you see me now, the hills did skip like rams, but it was Dickinson that told you so."

One evening at a dinner-party at Doctor Elrington's the conversation turned on Barrett. My father told a story of a gentleman who lived in a part of Dublin far from the College, who, on a very cold snowing night, had sent his son, a young boy, to Doctor Barrett's for a book which he had promised to lend him. The boy knocked at the door; Barrett came out of his room, in which there was no light, and on hearing what he wanted, went in again, leaving the boy shivering outside. He shortly returned with a book in his hand, and said, "Now, go home with this to your father, tell him I think it is the book he wants, for I think I can put my hand on every book in my library; but if it isn't, come back, do you see me now, and I'll light a candle and look for it." As my father finished, Elrington said, "Mr. Dean, I can vouch for the truth of that story, for *I* was that boy."

A student who lived in rooms on the floor below those of Doctor Barrett, and who knew what a miser he was, and that he would walk a mile any day to save or get a halfpenny, got one, bored a hole through it, and tied a long thin thread to it, then laid it on a step of the stairs, half-way between his rooms and Barrett's, and passed the thread under his own door, through a chink in which he watched for the approach of the doctor. The latter soon emerged from his room, and, as he came down the stairs, espied the halfpenny, and at once stooped to pick it up, when a gentle pull at the string brought it to the next step. There Barrett made another attempt to catch it; again it went to the next step; and so on to the bottom of the flight, eluding every grab the doctor made at it, till, by a sudden chuck at the thread, it disappeared altogether, passing under the student's door, while Barrett murmured, "Do you see me now, I never saw such a halfpenny as that!"

It is said that on his death his will was found to contain only the following words :—" I leave every thing I am possessed of to feed the hungry and clothe the naked." By the most penurious saving he had accumulated a considerable amount of money. Owing to the terms of his will legal difficulties arose as to its disposal, but I believe most of it ultimately went to his poor relations, who were many.

When residing near Dublin my father saw a good deal of Whately, who had recently been appointed Archbishop of Dublin in succession to Magee; he admired and liked him, and was often amused by his eccentricities, one of which was a wonderful way he had of throwing his legs about. The late Chief Justice Doherty told me that at the Privy Council he once put his hand into his pocket for his handkerchief; but instead of it found there the foot of the Archbishop, who happened that day to sit next him!

Judge Keogh told me that he was witness of the following scene:—The Archbishop had a large Newfoundland dog, of which he was very fond. He often took him into Stephen's Green, the large square opposite the palace, and there made him jump over a stick, fetch and carry, and do other tricks. One day, when thus engaged, he had just thrown a ball for the dog to fetch, when the following dialogue was heard between two women who were standing at the rails watching him:—

"Ah, then, Mary, do you know who that is playin' wid the dog?"

Mary. "Troth, I don't, Biddy; but he's a fine-lookin' man, whoever he is."

Biddy. "That's the archbishop, Mary."

Mary. "Do you tell me so? God bless the innocent craythur! Isn't he aisily amused?"

Biddy. "He's not our archbishop at all, Mary; he is the Protestant archbishop."

Mary. "Oh! the b—— ould fool."

It is well-known that he gave large sums in

charity, but made it a boast that on principle he had never given a farthing to a beggar in the streets. He used to tell of a beggar who followed him asking alms, to whom he said, " Go away ; I never give anything to a beggar in the streets." The beggar replied, " And where would your reverence wish me to wait on you ? "

At dinner parties, which he often gave to the clergy in his diocese, he was fond of propounding paradoxes, and as it was well known that he did not like any one to try to explain till he did so himself, it had become the custom not to hazard a remark, until it pleased his Grace to expound. At one of the parties he said in a loud voice, so as to be heard by all his guests, " Is it not strange that there should be no connection between religion and morality?" The usual silence of awe and curiosity which prevailed was, to the consternation of all, broken by a still louder voice from the lower end of the table, exclaiming, " If your Grace means that there are heathen religions which have no connection with morality, it is a truism; but if your Grace means that there is no connection between the Christian religion and morality, it is false." The offender was the Rev. John Jellett, a young clergyman, who had recently obtained a Fellowship in Dublin University, of which he was subsequently the distinguished Provost. He told me that it was some years before he was again invited to the palace.

Another time he asked, "Can any one tell me the vocative of cat?"

"O cat!" suggested a mild curate.

"Nonsense," said the Archbishop; "did any one ever say, 'O cat! come here'? Puss is the vocative."

Again he asked, "Is there any one here who is interested in ornithology? I ask because I was surprised, as I took a walk in the Phœnix Park to-day, to see a large number of fieldfares."

"A very rare bird, your Grace," said the Rev. Mr. A.

"Not at all, A.," said the Archbishop—"a very common bird indeed; but I was surprised to see them so early in the winter."

At another dinner party he asked, "Did any of you particularly observe the autumn tints this year?"

"I did, your Grace," said Mr. B.; "and most lovely they were."

"On the contrary," said his Grace, "I thought them about the poorest I ever saw in my life."

The last time I ever met Charles Lever (Harry Lorrequer) he told me that he and the Archbishop, accompanied by two curates, X. and Z., were taking a walk together in the Park, at a time when Whately was much exercised about mushrooms, as to what species were edible and wholesome, and what sorts poisonous. As they walked along, the Archbishop espied and picked up a dreadful looking brown and yellow fungus. "Now, Lever," he said, "many people might fancy that that is a poisonous fungus, while in reality no better or more wholesome mushroom grows." He thereupon broke off a bit of it, and handing it to Mr. X., said, "Try a bit, X., and tell us what you think of it."

"A very nice fungus, indeed, your Grace, and rather sweetish," said the Rev. Mr. X.

"Here's a bit for you, Z.; let us have your opinion of it."

"If it were nicely cooked, your Grace," said the Rev. Mr. Z., making a very wry face, "with a little salt and butter, it would, I am sure, be delicious."

Whately then, handing a piece of it to Lever, said, "Here, Lever, try a bit, and say what *you* think of it."

"I thank your Grace, I'd rather not," said he. "'Tis true I have a brother in the Church, but he is not in your Grace's diocese."

CHAPTER VII.

The "Charleys'" life was not a pleasant one—Paddy O'Neill and his rhymes—"With my rigatooria"—Too far west to wash—On the coast at Kilkee—"Phaudrig Crohoore"—The *Dublin Magazine*.

WHEN I was in college a favourite amusement of the ingenious youth there was tormenting the old city watchmen, or "Charleys" as they were called. They were the only guardians of the city by night; there were none by day; the metropolitan police did not then exist. These watchmen were generally old and often feeble. Many of them had in their earlier days been the domestic servants or retainers of members of the Corporation and of their friends. They wore long grey frieze coats, with large capes and low-crowned hats. Their only weapon, offensive and defensive, was what was called a crook, a long pole with a spear at the end, and near the spear a crook for catching runaway offenders. They also carried a rattle, which, when whirled swiftly round, made a loud, harsh, and grating sound like the voice of a gigantic corncrake; with this, when in trouble or in danger, they summoned other watchmen to their assistance. To rob them of these was an exploit not to be despised. In the college rooms of friends of mine—some of them afterwards judges, others eminent divines—I have seen, hanging up as trophies, many a crook and many a rattle.

The duties of these ancient guardians of the peace were, to patrol a certain beat, to quell riots, and to arrest and bring to the watch-house disorderly characters. They had also, as they walked along their beat, to call out the hour and the state of the weather—" Past twelve o'clock, and a cloudy night!" or " Past two o'clock, and a stormy morning!" as the case might be. They were not very attentive to their duties, and spent a great part of their time in sleeping snugly in their watch-boxes, which were much like soldiers' sentry-boxes, but more comfortable; and how often, after a cosy doze, has a poor fellow woke up from his pleasant dreams to find his crook and rattle gone!

To catch a "Charley" fast asleep, and to overturn his watch-box, face downward on the ground, was the grandest feat of all. When in this position his rattle could not be heard at any distance, and his assailants were wont to let him lie in that helpless state for a considerable time before they turned the box over on its side and let him out. Before he was on his legs they were far out of reach of capture.

A cousin of mine, Brinsley H——, a remarkably steady youth, who highly disapproved of these attacks on the old men, and, amongst his other good qualities, had, or thought he had, a mission to see that all men with whom he came in contact did their duty in their respective callings, was coming home late one night, and as he passed a watch-box was attracted by the sound of snoring. On looking in he saw the occupant in profound slumber. He roused him up at once, and said, "You ought to be ashamed of yourself, asleep in your box and neglecting your duty. If I hadn't wakened you, you would probably have lost your crook and your rattle. I shall certainly report you to the city magistrate to-morrow morning." "Bedad, then," said the Charley, "I'll report you first, my boy," and seizing him by the collar, he sprung his rattle, and held him till two other watchmen arrived. The three of them then conveyed him to the watch-house, where he was kept till ten o'clock next morning, when he was brought before Mr. Cole, one of the city magistrates. The watchman swore that the young gentleman had assaulted him, and tried to wrest his crook from him; the other men gave evidence of his violent conduct and abusive language as they led him to the watch-house. Mr. Cole asked him what he had to say for himself. H—— told the true story, exactly as it happened. The magistrate did not seem to attach much credence to it; but, as he had been all night in a cell, dismissed him with a caution, saying, "I hope, young man, that this will be a warning to you, and that you will not again behave in such a way; and I promise you that if you are ever brought before me for an offence of this sort again, I shall deal severely with you. You may go now." I never saw a man so indignant as Brinsley was when he next day told me of his wrongs, and of the cruel injustice of Mr. Cole. From that day he never again roused a sleeping watchman, but acted on the wise principle of letting sleeping dogs lie. Though over eighty, he is hale and hearty still, and if this should meet his eye he will smile at the recollection of his early wrongs.

After our return to Abington we occasionally spent a few weeks in summer at Kilkee, in the county of Clare, now a much-frequented watering-place, then a wild village on the wildest coast of Ireland. A new steamboat, the *Garry Owen*, had then begun to ply between Limerick and Kilrush, a considerable town, about eight miles from Kilkee. On the voyage, which generally took about four hours—sometimes five or more if the weather was bad—the passengers were cheered by the music and songs of a famous character, one Paddy O'Neill, whose playing on the fiddle was only surpassed by his performances on the bagpipes. He was, moreover, a poet, and sang his own songs with vigour and expression to his own accompaniment. One of these songs was in praise of the new steamboat, and was in the style of the well-known song, "*Garry Owen*," which, as most Irishmen know, begins in this fashion—

"Oh, *Garry Owen* is gone to wrack,
　　Since Johnny O'Connell is gone to Cork,
Though Paddy O'Brien jumped out of the dock,
　　In spite of judge and jury.
'Twas in Irishtown a battle begun,
'Twas down the Mall he made them run,
'Twas in *Garry Owen* we had the fun,
　　On Easter Tuesday morning."

I regret that I only remember the first verse of Paddy's song. It ran thus—

"Oh, *Garry Owen* is no more a wrack;
Whoever says she is, is a noted ass;
She's an iron boat that flies like shot
　　Against the strongest storm.
On Kilrush Quay there's brave O'Brien,
Of ancient line, without spot or slime;
In double quick time, with graceful smile,
　　He hands ashore the ladies."

It will be seen that in these verses, as in most Irish songs, it is the vowels that make the rhyme. In the former, "wrack," "Cork," and "dock," and in the latter "wrack," "ass," and "shot," are made to rhyme. In another of Paddy's songs, "A Parody on the famous rebel song, 'The Shan Van Vocht,'" the following rhymes appear:—

"We'll have turkeys and roast beef,
And we'll eat them very sweet,
And then will take a sleep,
　　Says the Shan Van Vocht."

One summer evening my brother, who was a prime favourite of his, persuaded Paddy to drive across with him from Kilrush to Kilkee, and there they got up a dance in Mrs. Reade's lodge, where some of our family were sojourning at the time. I am sorry to say I was away somewhere and missed the fun. The dance music was supplied by Paddy's pipes and fiddle, and between the dances he sang some of his favourite songs. Next day my brother wrote some doggerel verses celebrating the dance and in imitation of the "Wedding of Ballyporean," a song then very popular in the south of Ireland. One verse ran—

"But Paddy no longer his fiddle could twig,
And the heat was so great that he pulled off his wig;
But Mary McCarthy being still for a jig,
He screwed his old pipes till they roared like a pig.
  Oh! they fell to their dancing once more, sir,
  Till their marrow bones all grew quite sore, sir,
  And they were obliged to give o'er, sir,
    At the dance in the lodge at Kilkee."

A copy of the verses was presented to Paddy, who was highly delighted with them, and for years after sang them with much applause to the passengers on the *Garry Owen*. A few days after the dance he came to see my brother, and said he would be for ever obliged to him if he would alter one little word in the song.

"Of course I shall, with pleasure," said my brother. "What is the word?"

"Pig, your honour," said Paddy. "I'm sure your honour doesn't think my beautiful pipes sounded like a pig."

"Oh," he answered, "you don't think I meant

JOSEPH SHERIDAN LE FANU.

that they sounded like the grunt or squeak of a pig? I only meant that they were as loud as a pig."

"As loud as a pig!" said Paddy, rather indignantly; "as loud as a pig! They wor a great deal louder; but if your honour wouldn't mind changing that one word, I think it would be a great improvement, and would sound more natural like. This is the way I'd like it to go—

'But Mary McCarthy being still for a jig,
He scrowed his old pipes till they roar'd like a nymph.'

You see, your honour, the rhyme would be just as good, and I think it would be more like the rale tune of it."

The suggested improvement was at once made, to Paddy's great satisfaction.

My brother told me that it was a favourite song of Paddy's that suggested to him the plot of "Shamus O'Brien." Here is the song—

"I am a young man that never yet was daunted;
I always had money, plenty, when I wanted;
Courting pretty fair maids was all the trade I'd folly:
My life I would venture for you, my sporting Molly.

"As I was going up the Galtee mountain
I met with Captain Pepper; his money he was counting.
I first drew out my pistol, and then drew out my weapon:
'Stand and deliver, for I am the receiver.'

"When I got the money—it was a nice penny—
I put it in my pocket, and brought it home to Molly.
Molly, she told me she never would decave me;
But the divil's in the women, for they never can be 'asy.

"I went to her chamber for to take a slumber;
I went to her chamber—sure, I thought it little wonder.
I took out my pistols, and laid them on the table;
She discharged off them both, and filled them up with water.

"Early next morning, between six and seven,
The guard they surrounded me, with brave Captain Ledwell.
I ran to my pistols, but sure I was mistaken;
I discharged off the water, and a prisoner I was taken.

"Johnny, oh, Johnny, you are a gallant soldier;
You carry your firelock over your shoulder.
When you meet those gentlemen you're sure to make them tremble:
Put your whistle to your mouth, and your party will assemble.

"Johnny, oh, Johnny, I oftentimes told you,
With your bright shining sword, how the guard would surround you;
With your silver-mounted pistols deluding pretty fair maids,
Which causes your head to lie under the raven.

"I have two brothers 'listed in the army;
One is in Killiney, the other in Killarney.
If I had them here, I would be brave and charming.
I'd rather have them here than you, my sporting Molly.

"I stood in the hall while the turnkey was brawling;
I stood in the hall while the roll it was calling.
'Twas with my metal bolt I knocked the sentry down;
I made my escape, adieu to Nenagh town.
    With my rigatooria,
    Right, foltheladdy; with my rigatooria."

The chorus, "With my rigatooria," etc., which I have appended only to the last verse, was sung by Paddy, with much expression, at the end of each verse, and, in his opinion, greatly added to the effect and beauty of the song.

The cliffs at Kilkee, though not so high as some others on the west coast of Ireland, are amongst the boldest; they overhang so much, that if from the highest of them, Look-out Hill, you drop a stone over the edge, it falls well out into the sea. A stranger will hardly venture to look over the top of the cliff without kneeling or lying down; while the natives will sit quite happily on the very edge, with their legs dangling over, as they fish with long hand-lines for rock bream in the sea below. This, of course, they can do only on fine days; in stormy weather the foam and spray of the great Atlantic waves are driven right over the top of the cliffs.

In those days bathing on the strand in the Bay of Kilkee was carried out in a rather primitive style. A shower-bath was given by a man who climbed up at the back of the bath, carrying a bucket full of water, which he poured through a colander on the bather. A lady had taken her place in the bath, quite ready for the shower, when she heard a voice say to her, through the colander, "If you'd be plazed, my lady, to stand a little more to the west, I'd be able to give it to you better."

In the south of Ireland they constantly speak of a man being gone west or east, but never north or south. For instance, if in Kenmare you happened to ask where a man had gone, they would say, "To Killarney," or "To Glangarriff," as the case might be, but never "North to Killarney," or "South to Glengarriff." However, if he had gone to Sneem, or to Kilgarvin, they would invariably say, "He's gone west to Sneem," or "East to Kilgarvin." "West" is also used to mean back or backwards. When at our fishing quarters in Kerry some years ago, a small peasant boy, Davy Cronin by name, unwashed and unkempt, with hands and face as black as a potato-pot, used to come and sit near us on the bank of the river. My wife told him that unless he washed and made himself clean, she could not let him sit near our children. Next day he appeared with his face and hands much cleaner, but with the back of his neck as black as ever. "You are a good boy, Davy," said my wife to him, "to have washed your hands and face; but when you were about it, why didn't you wash the back of your neck?" "'Twas too far west, my lady," was the answer.

Another day, Jim Shea, who was then my fishing attendant, had a violent fit of coughing. "I'll give you something this evening," said my wife, "that will do your cold good." "'Tis not a cold I have at all, my lady," said he; "'tis a fly that's gone west in my stomach."

This last word reminds me of a story, told me by a friend, of a little girl, a niece of his, who had been told by her mother that "stomach" was not a nice word, and that a young lady ought not to use it. Some time afterwards she had done something naughty, and was put into the corner, and told to stay there till she was good. As no sign of penitence appeared, her mother took the initiative, and said, "Well, Mary, are you good now?" "No," said she, "I'm not good. Stomach — stomach — stomach—stomach!"

Kilkee has been for many years a favourite summer resort of the people of Limerick and the neighbouring counties; I wonder it is not more often visited by tourists from other parts of the country, and from England. The scenery is magnificently wild, the cliffs, many hundred feet high, go sheer down to the sea, many of them even overhanging.

No vessel willingly approaches this iron-bound coast, and in the many times I have been there I do not think I have seen a sail half a dozen times, and when I did see one it was far away in the offing. One winter, on Christmas morning, the *Intrinsic*, having been disabled at sea, was driven by the storm under the highest of the cliffs, where she came to anchor, and there for hours she lay battered and buffeted by the waves. Crowds collected on the Look-out Hill which overhung the cliff. The coast-guard men were there, trying in vain, with rockets, to send a rope to the ship. Two or three times in the forenoon some of the crew were seen on deck; two of them were washed overboard and lost; after midday none were seen. From hour to hour the crowd increased. The priests from Kilkee came up and celebrated Mass on the hill, while the people knelt, in the storm and rain, praying for those in peril on the ship. The Mass had scarcely ended when a huge wave struck the vessel; she heeled over and sunk. A gull was seen to pick up something from the sea where she went down, which, when flying high overhead, it dropped amongst the crowd; it was a lady's glove. The captain's wife had perished with her husband and the crew.

Years after this, in November 1850, professional business brought me for a day to Kilkee. The greatest storm known for years had been raging for the two previous days. It was a grand sight, those mighty Atlantic waves dashing and breaking against the rocks, and sending foam and spray flying high above the lofty cliffs. The day before I arrived, an emigrant ship, the *Edmund*, had left Limerick for America, with between two and three hundred emigrants on board, and on the following night had been caught in this great storm. A ledge, called the Dugarna Rocks, stretches a great part of the way across the mouth of the little Bay of Kilkee; over this she was carried by the waves, and driven right up to the village, her bows high and dry on the rocks close to the coastguard station. The greater number of the passengers were saved, but about a hundred of them were still on board when the vessel went to pieces; they were drowned, and with them the ship's carpenter, a brave fellow, who had risked his life again and again in saving some of the emigrants, and had gone on board once more to rescue others. I saw lying side by side, on a sail spread on the beach, many of the poor drowned ones, most of them young women and children; others were constantly being washed ashore and were laid with those already there. Had I not seen it I would not have believed that such a large vessel could have so completely broken up in so short a time; all that was left of her were fragments scattered on the rocks and beach. That night I had a long and weary journey from Kilkee to Limerick, over sixty miles, on an outside car in storm and rain, and could think of nothing all through the night but the terrible scene I had witnessed, and ever before me were the poor sad faces I had seen upon the sail.

In 1839 my brother became connected with the *Dublin University Magazine*, of which he was subsequently the proprietor; to it he contributed the many interesting and amusing Irish stories, afterwards collected in the *Purcell Papers*. Some of them I used occasionally to recite, and wishing to have one in verse, I asked him to write one for me. He said he did not know what subject I would like. I said, "Give me an Irish Young Lochinvar," and in a few days he sent me "Phaudrig Crohoore" ("Patrick Connor;" or, more correctly, "Patrick the Son of Connor"). Although it has appeared in the *Purcell Papers*, my readers may not object to see it here.

PHAUDRIG CROHOORE.

"Oh! Phaudrig Crohoore was the broth of a boy,
 An' he stood six foot eight;
 An' his arm was as round as another man's thigh—
 'Tis Phaudrig was great.

An' his hair was as black as the shadows of night—
An' hung over the scars left by many a fight;
An' his voice, like the thunder, was deep, strong, and loud,
An' his eye like the lightning from under the cloud.
An' all the girls liked him, for he could spake civil,
An' sweet when he liked it, for he was the divil.
An' there wasn't a girl from thirty-five under,
Divil a matter how cross, but he could come round her.
But of all the sweet girls that smiled on him but one
Was the girl of his heart, an' he loved her alone;
For warm as the sun, as the rock firm and sure,
Was the love of the heart of Phaudrig Crohoore.
An' he'd die for one smile from his Kathleen O'Brien,
For his love, like his hatred, was strong as the lion.

" But Michael O'Hanlon loved Kathleen as well
As he hated Crohoore, an' that same was like hell.
But O'Brien liked him, for they were the same parties,
The O'Briens, O'Hanlons, and Murphys, and Cartys;
An' they all went together and hated Crohoore,
For it's many's the batin' he gave them before;
An' O'Hanlon made up to O'Brien, an' says he,
'I'll marry your daughter, if you'll give her to me.'
An' the match was made up, an' when Shrovetide came on,
The company assembled three hundred, if one.
There was all the O'Hanlons, an' Murphys, an' Cartys,
An' the young boys an' girls of all of them parties.
The O'Briens, of coorse, gathered strong on that day,
An' the pipers an' fiddlers were tearin' away;
There was roarin', an' jumpin', an' jiggin', an' flingin',
An' jokin', an' blessin', an' kissin', an' singin';
An' they wor all laughin'—why not to be sure?—
How O'Hanlon come inside of Phaudrig Crohoore;
An' they talked an' they laughed the length of the table,
'Atin' an' drinkin' all while they were able;
An' with pipin' an' fiddlin', an' roarin' like thunder,
Your head you'd think fairly was splittin' asunder.
An' the priest called out, 'Silence, ye blackguards, agin,'
An' he took up his prayer-book, just goin' to begin.
An' they all held their tongues from their funnin' an' bawlin',
So silent you'd notice the smallest pin fallin'.

An' the priest was just beginnin' to read, when the door
Sprang back to the wall, an' in walked Crohoore.
Oh! Phaudrig Crohoore was the broth of a boy,
  An' he stood six foot eight;
An' his arm was as round as another man's thigh—
  'Tis Phaudrig was great.
An' he walked slowly up, watched by many a bright eye,
As a black cloud moves on through the stars of the sky;
An' none strove to stop him, for Phaudrig was great,
Till he stood, all alone, just opposite the sate
Where O'Hanlon and Kathleen, his beautiful bride,
Were sittin' so illigant out side by side.
An' he gave her one look that her heart almost broke,
An' he turned to O'Brien, her father, and spoke;
An' his voice, like the thunder, was deep, strong, and loud,
An' his eye shone like lightning from under the cloud.

"'I didn't come here like a tame, crawlin' mouse,
But I stand like a man in my enemies' house.
In the field, on the road, Phaudrig never knew fear
Of his foemen, an' God knows he scorns it here;
So lave me at aise, for three minutes or four,
To spake to the girl I'll never see more.'
And to Kathleen he turned, an' his voice changed its tone,
For he thought of the days when he called her his own,
An' his eye blazed like lightnin' from under the cloud
On his false-hearted girl, reproachful an' proud.
An' says he, 'Kathleen bawn, is it true what I hear,
That you marry of your free choice, without threat or fear?
If so, spake the word, an' I'll turn an' depart,
Cheated once, an' once only, by woman's false heart.'

"Oh! sorrow an' love made the poor girl dumb,
An' she tried hard to spake, but the words wouldn't come;
For the sound of his voice, as he stood there fornint her,
Went cold on her heart, as the night wind in winter;
An' the tears in her blue eyes stood tremblin' to flow,
An' pale was her cheek, as the moonshine on snow.

"Then the heart of bold Phaudrig swelled high in its place,
For he knew, by one look in that beautiful face,

That, though strangers and foemen their pledged hands might
   sever,
Her true heart was his, an' his only, for ever.
An' he lifted his voice like the eagle's hoarse call,
An' says Phaudrig, 'She's mine still, in spite of you all!'
Then up jumped O'Hanlon—an' a tall boy was he—
An' he looked on bold Phaudrig as fierce as could be;
An' says he, 'By the holy, before you go out,
Bold Phaudrig Crohoore, you must fight for a bout.'
Then Phaudrig made answer, 'I'll do my endeavour;'
An' with one blow he stretched bold O'Hanlon for ever.
In his arms he took Kathleen, and stepped to the door,
An' he leaped on his horse, an' he flung her before.
An' they all were so bothered that not a man stirred
Till the galloping hoofs on the pavement were heard;
Then up they all started, like bees in the swarm,
An' they riz a great shout, like the burst of a storm;
An' they roared, an' they ran, an' they shouted galore;
But Kathleen an' Phaudrig they never saw more.

"But them days are gone by, an' he is no more,
An' the green grass is growin' o'er Phaudrig Crohoore;
For he couldn't be aisy or quiet at all;
As he lived a brave boy, he resolved so to fall.
An' he took a good pike, for Phaudrig was great,
An' he fought, an' he died in the year ninety-eight;
An' the day that Crohoore in the green field was killed,
A strong boy was stretched, an' a strong heart was stilled."

When Phaudrig Crohoore appeared in the *Dublin University Magazine*, my brother, under his *nom de plume*, wrote a preface to it, in which he said that it had been composed by a poor Irish minstrel, Michael Finley, who could neither read nor write, but used to recite it, with others of his songs and ballads, at fairs and markets.

Many years afterwards, one evening, after I

had recited it at Lord Spencer's, who was then Lord Lieutenant of Ireland, the late primate, Beresford, said to Lady Spencer, who was sitting near me, "I can tell you a curious fact, Lady Spencer; that poem was composed by a poor Irish peasant, one Michael Finley, who could neither read nor write." Then turning to me, "Were you aware of that, Mr. Le Fanu?" "I was, your Grace," said I; "and you may be surprised to hear that I knew the Michael Finley who wrote the ballad intimately—he was, in fact, my brother. But in one particular your Grace is mistaken; he could read and write a little." The primate took it very well, and was much amused.

Some of my brother's earliest stories in the *University Magazine* abound in fun about courtship and matrimony. In one he makes the narrator, an Irish peasant, thus describe the condition of Billy Malowney when courting pretty Molly Donovan. "Well, now, he was raly stupid wid love; there wasn't a bit of fun left in him. He was good for nothing on earth but sittin' under bushes smokin' tobaccy and sighing, till you'd wonder where he got the wind for it all. Now you might as well be persuadin' the birds again' flying, or strivin' to coax the stars out of the sky into your hat, as to be talking common sense to them that's fairly bothered and burstin' wid love. There is nothing like it. The toothache and colic together would compose you better for an argument; it leaves you fit for nothing but nonsinse. It's stronger than whisky, for one good drop of it will make you drunk for a year, and sick, begorra, for ten; it's stronger than the sea, for it will carry you round the world, and never let you sink in sunshine or in storm; and, begorra, it's stronger than Death itself, for it's not afear'd of him, but dares him in every shape. But lovers does have their quarrels sometimes; and, begorra, when they do, you'd almost think they hated one another like man and wife."

Another time he makes a man warn his son against matrimony, telling him that "marriage is like the smallpox. A man may have it mildly, but he generally carries the marks of it with him to his grave."

In another story he puts into the mouth of an Irish farmer, addressing his son, the following cynical view of life, the last part of which very considerably shocked the Dean:—

"You see, my boy, a man's life naturally divides itself into three distinct periods. The first is that in which he is plannin' and conthrivin' all sorts of villainy and rascality; that is the period of youth and innocence. The second is that in which he is puttin' into practice the villainy and rascality he contrived before; that is the prime of life or the flower of manhood. The third and last period is that in which he is makin' his soul and preparin' for another world; that is the period of dotage."

CHAPTER VIII.

Peasant life after the famine of 1847—An aged goose—Superstitions and Irish peculiarities—The worship of Baal—The Blarney stone — The wren boys — The direful "wurrum"—A remedy for the chin cough, and doctors' remedies.

UNTIL after the famine of 1847 there was but little change in the mode of life of the people, or in the wages of workmen. When we went to the south the pay of labourers was sevenpence a day; the farmers accused my father of spoiling the market by giving his men ninepence. The peasants, except the few who had land enough to keep a cow, lived altogether on potatoes, with which on rare occasions they had a salt herring or two. Milk they could not get, for when—which was very seldom indeed—they could have afforded to buy it the farmers would not sell it, as they wanted it to feed their calves. The potatoes were boiled in a huge iron pot, from which they were thrown into a big open-work wicker basket, shaped like the bowl of a spoon; this was placed over another large pot or over a trough, till the water was thoroughly drained off; the potatoes were then turned out on the middle of the table in a heap. There was sometimes a coarse tablecloth, more often none. There were no knives or forks, nor any plates, but one on which the herring, if one was there, lay. From time to time each one of the family nipped with finger and thumb a little bit of the herring, to give a flavour to his "pratee." Meat they never tasted except on Christmas Day and Easter Sunday; but all, no matter how poor, managed to have a bit of meat of some sort on these days.

As I drove from Limerick one Christmas Eve an elderly woman with a small bundle in her hand ran after the car, holding on to the back of it. I got into conversation with her, and after some other talk I asked her what she had in her bundle.

" 'Tis some *cus-a-muck* (pigs' feet) I have, your honour, for Christmas." After a pause she added, " I got them for the price of a goose I sold in Limerick to-day."

" Wouldn't the goose," said I, " have been better for dinner than the pigs' feet?"

" Av course it would, your honour, if we could ate her."

" Why couldn't you?" said I.

" She was too ould and tough, your honour. I'm married twenty-five years ago last Shrove, and she was an ould goose then; and I'd never have sold her, only she was stoppin' of layin' by rason of her ould age." She then began to laugh heartily, and said, "It's what I'm laughing at, your honour, thinking of them that bought her, how they'll be breakin' the back of their heads against the wall to-morrow, strivin' with their teeth to pull the mate off her ould bones!"

It would take volumes to tell of all the old customs and superstitions of the peasantry. Many of them have died out, and others are rapidly dying. Here I shall only mention a few of them.

On St. John's Eve, the 23rd of June, still may be seen a few bonfires on the mountains; in the old days they blazed on every hill and in every farm. No field was fruitful into which a burning brand had not been thrown, no horse or cow which had not been touched by fire on that night.

This custom had its origin in pre-Christian times, as the name of the fires, Baal thinna (Baal's fires), shows. It is more than a hundred years since the late Rev. Donald Macqueen, of Kilmuir, in the Isle of Skye, visited Ireland; in the account of his tour, he says that "The Irish have ever been worshippers of fire and of Baal, and are so to this day. The chief festival in honour of the sun and fire is upon the 21st of June, when the sun arrives at the summer solstice, or rather begins its retrograde motion." Then follows the description of the Baal fires which he saw.

"I was so fortunate in the summer of 1782 as to have my curiosity gratified. At the house where I was entertained it was told me that we should see at midnight the most singular sight in Ireland, which was the lighting of fires in honour of the sun. Accordingly, exactly at midnight, the fires

began to appear; and going up to the leads of the
house, which had a widely extended view, I saw,
on a radius of thirty miles, all round the fires burning on every eminence which the country afforded.
I had a further satisfaction of learning, from un-
doubted authority, that the people danced round the
fires, and at the close went through these fires, and
made their sons and daughters, together with their
cattle, pass through the fire, and the whole was
concluded with religious solemnity."

There is another Irish phrase ("Baal-o-yerib!")
connected with the worship of Baal. But before I
go further I had better confess that I am not an
Irish scholar; and although I know the meaning of
a great many Irish words, I do not know how to
spell one of them. Any I give I have spelt
phonetically, as nearly as I can in the way I heard
them spoken by the peasantry. I believe this will
give a better idea how they sound when spoken than
if I had been able to write them correctly; for any
Irish words which I have happened to see, written
by those who know the language, do not bear the
slightest resemblance to the same words when spoken.

But to return to our "Baal-o-yerib!"—it was and,
where Irish is spoken, still is the salutation addressed
by any one passing by to men working in a field, or,
on entering a house, to the inmates, who reply,
"Dhe-as-macra-guth!" None of the peasantry whom
I have asked could give me a translation of this
salutation; they said they thought it meant " God

bless the work!" or "God save all here!" They all knew what the reply means. The late Rev. Patrick Fitzgerald, a good Irish scholar, told me that "Baal-o-yerib!" means "Baal, or God, be with you!" and was originally used when there were worshippers of Baal still in Ireland. The reply of a Christian, "Dhe-as-maera-guth!" means "God and Mary be with you!" In recent times, where Irish has died out, the salutation is changed to "God bless the work!" or "God save all here!" as the case may be, to which the reply is, "God save you kindly!"

I have seen it told in an Irish story—one of Mrs. S. C. Hall's, I think—that a peasant, on entering a house, says, "God bless all here, barrin' the dog and the cat!" This is, I believe, a complete mistake. I have never heard it said, nor have I met any one who has. It is, however, founded on the fact that the peasantry will never say, "God bless it!" to a dog or cat, though they do say it to everything else, animate or inanimate. Of a child they would say, "That's a nice child; God bless it!" of a pig, "That's a nate pig; God bless it!" or of a gun, "That's a beautiful piece; God bless it!" but of a dog or cat only "That's a great dog," or "That's a purty cat," but never "God bless it!" indeed, they would think it profane in the highest degree to say so. An English friend who was staying with us, but did not know of this exception, wishing to make himself agreeable to a countryman who showed him a dog, said, "That's a fine dog; God bless him!" I shall never forget the expression of that peasant's face. He said nothing, but devoutly crossed himself.

I have seen in the same or some other story a similar mistake, where a peasant is made to say to some one who sneezes, "God bless you, barrin' it's the snuff!" They would never say so. If one sneezes in a natural way, they always say, "God bless you!" but if the sneeze is caused by snuff, or any other artificial means, they never bless the sneezer.

When speaking of the Baal fires, I should have said that fire is a great protection against fairies. Whenever churning is going on, a small bit of burning turf is put under the churn to prevent the abstraction of the butter by the "good people."

Another custom is, that any one coming into a house where churning is going on must take the churn-dash and churn for a few seconds. His doing this prevents a person with an evil eye, should any such come in, charming away the butter or otherwise spoiling the churning.

The belief in magpies still prevails. It is lucky to see two, unlucky to see one. The ill results from seeing only one can be mitigated, sometimes altogether escaped, by taking off your hat and bowing to the bird. This belief and custom is not very old in Ireland, as it is not so very long since the magpie was first introduced here. Holinshed, when speaking of birds in Ireland, says, "They also lacke the bird called the pie."

There are, I fear, few who still believe that after a dip in the Shannon the bather will never blush again.

The Blarney stone too, I am afraid, is going out of date. In former days, whoever kissed it was at once endowed with the gift of the blarney, as the old song, "The Groves of Blarney," tells us.

> " 'Tis there's the stone that whoever kisses
> He never misses to grow eloquent;
> 'Tis he may clamber to a lady's chamber,
> Or become a member of Parliament.
>
> "A noble spouter he'll sure turn out, or
> An out and outer to be let alone;
> Don't try to hinder him, or to bewilder him,
> For he is a pilgrim from the Blarney stone."

But many, especially ladies, who climbed to the top of the old castle for the express purpose of kissing the Blarney stone, found that none of these good results followed. But why? Their guide, to save himself and them trouble, had made them kiss the wrong stone—a little stone in the corner of the tower, which has no virtue whatever.

The real stone, which I am proud to say I kissed many a year ago, is about four feet below the parapet on the outside of the castle. To kiss it, you must be held by the legs, head downwards, over the battlements.

The "wren boys," on Saint Stephen's Day, still drag on a poor and miserable existence. Half a dozen ragged urchins, carrying a little bit of holly, with a wren, or more often some other little dead bird, tied to it, come to the hall door begging for halfpence. In former days, in the south, one of the Christmas amusements, which we looked forward to with pleasure, was the visit of the wren boys, or "mummers," as they sometimes called themselves. There were generally twelve or fourteen of them, fine strapping young fellows, between eighteen and five and twenty years of age; they were dressed in their Sunday's best, with many-coloured ribbons in their hats, and scarfs across their breasts. One of them carried the holly bush, also adorned with ribbons, on top of which was the wren. Another was dressed up as the *aumadhawn*, or fool; his coat was a sack, with holes in it for his head, legs, and arms to come through; his head-dress was a hare-skin, and on his face he wore a hideous mask; in his hand he carried a stick with a bladder tied to the end of it. His duty was to keep order. This he did by whacking all offenders with this weapon. The party was accompanied by a piper or a fiddler, often by both; they were followed by a crowd of country boys and girls, whom the aumadhawn kept at a respectful distance. Thus equipped and accompanied, they visited the houses of the gentry and strong farmers.

The entertainment began by the singing of the wren song, of which I remember only the following verse:—

> "The wren, the wren, the king of all birds,
> Saint Stephen's Day, was caught in the furze;
> Although he is little, his family's great,
> Rise up, lords and ladies, and give us a treat."

Then came the dancing of merry jigs and reels. There was no lack of partners for the boys; amongst them were the young ladies of the house and the servant-maids, not to mention the pretty girls in the crowd that followed them. When they had had refreshments, or a present of money wherewith to get them, off they went, with three hearty cheers for the master and mistress of the house.

The dreadful beast, the "wurrum," half fish, half dragon, still survives in many a mountain lake—seldom seen indeed, but often heard. Near our fishing quarters in Kerry there are two such lakes; one, the beautiful little lake at the head of the Blackwater river, called Lough Brin, from Brin, or Bran, as he is now called, the direful wurrum which inhabits it. The man who minds the boat there, speaks with awe of Bran; he tells me he has never seen him, and hopes he never may, but has often heard him roaring on a stormy night. On being questioned as to what the noise was like, he said it was like the roaring of a young bull. To my suggestion that perhaps "it might have been a young bull," he made no reply, but the expression of his face showed what he thought of the levity, or perhaps even the irreverence, of the remark.

Some miles further on, between Lough Brin and Glencar, there is another lake, from which two years ago a boy, while bathing, was driven and chased by the dreadful wurrum which dwells in it. It bit him on the back, and hunted him all the way home, where he arrived naked and bleeding; he had not waited even to take up his clothes. On being asked what the beast was like, he said, " 'Twas something like the form of a donkey." What may have really happened to the boy we have never been able to discover.

On the opposite side of Kenmare Bay is still to be seen one of these wurrums of enormous size. It was slain by St. Patrick, and turned into stone, and, as a worm-like ledge of rock, now winds along the side of Coom na Peastha ("the Valley of the Worm"). St. Patrick, as is well known, banished all venomous and poisonous creatures from Ireland. His feats in this direction are celebrated in the well-known song in his praise, in the following verses:—

> "Nine hundred thousand vipers blue
> He charmed with sweet discourses,
> And dined on them at Killaloe
> In soups and second courses.
> When blind worms, crawling through the grass,
> Disgusted all the nation,
>   He gave them a rise
>   That opened their eyes
> To a sense of their situation.

> " There's not a mile in Ireland's isle
> Where dirty vermin musters
> But there he put his neat fore-foot,
> And murdered them in clusters.
>   The frogs went hop,
>   The toads went flop,
> Splash, dash into the water;
>   The snakes committed suicide
> To save themselves from slaughter.

> "Oh, success attend Saint Patrick's fist,
> For he's the saint so clever;
> He gave the snakes and toads a twist,
> And bothered them for ever."

Notwithstanding all this, there still exists a species of toad (the natchet, I think) in the barony of Iveragh, in the west of Kerry. I was fishing in the Carah river the first time I saw them. I said to two countrymen, who were standing by, "How was it that these toads escaped Saint Patrick?" "Well, now, yer honour," said one of them, "it's what I'm tould that when Saint Patrick was down in these parts he went up the Reeks, and when he seen what a wild and disolute place Iveragh was, he wouldn't go any further; and that's the rason them things does be here still." "Well now, yer honour," said the other fellow, "I wouldn't altogether give in to that, for av coorse the saint was, many's the time, in worse places than Iveragh. It's what I hear, yer honour, that it was a lady that sent them from England in a letter fifty or sixty years ago."

Possibly they may have been imported. I know that many attempts have been made to introduce snakes and vipers into Ireland—happily, so far, unsuccessfully.

Of the effect of the soil of Ireland on toads and snakes, Holinshed, in his "Chronicles," gives the following anecdotes:—

"Certeine merchants affirme, that when they had

unladen their ships, in Ireland, they found, by hap, some toads under their balast. And they had no sooner cast them on the shore, than they would puffe and swell unmeasurablie, and shortlie after turning up their bellies, they would burst in sunder.

"And not onlie the earth and dust of Ireland, but also the verie thongs of Irish leather have the verie same force and virtue. I have seene it, saith Cambrensis, experimented, that a toad being incompassed with a thong of Irish leather, and creeping thitherward, indevoring to have skipt over it, suddenlie reculed backe, as though it had beene rapt in the head; whereupon it began to sprall to the other side. But at length perceiving that the thong did embaie it of all parts, it began to thirle, and as it were to dig the earth, where finding an hole, it slunke awaie in the presence of sundrie persons.

"It happened also in my time, saith Giraldus Cambrensis, that in the north of England a knot of yongkers tooke a nap in the fields: as one of them laie snorting with his mouth gaping, as though he would have caught flies, it happened that a snake or adder slipt into his mouth, and glided down into his bellie, where harboring itselfe, it began to roame up and downe, and to feede on the yoong man his entrals. The patient being sore distracted and above measure tormented with the biting pangs of this greedie ghest, incessantlie praied to God, that if it stood with His gratious will, either wholie to bereave him of his life, or else of his unspeakable mercie to ease him of his paine. The worme would never ceasse from gnawing the patient his carcasse, but when he had taken his repast, and his meat was no sooner digested, than it would give a fresh onset in boring his guts. Diverse remidies were sought, and medicins, pilgrimages to saints, but all could not prevaile. Being at length schooled by the grave advice of some sage and expert father, that willed him to make his speedie repair to Ireland, would tract no time, but busked himselfe over sea and arrived in Ireland. He did no sooner drinke of the water of that Iland, and taken of the vittels of Ireland, but he forthwith kild the snake, and so being lustie and livelie, he returned into England." Holinshed goes on to say, "There be some that move question, whether the want of venemous wormes in Ireland be to be imputed to the propertie of the soile, or to be ascribed to the praiers of Saint Patrike, who converted that Iland. The greater part father it on Saint Patrike, especiallie such as write his life as well apart, as in the legend of Irish saints."

There are still in Ireland two small creatures which the saint might as well have abolished when his hand was in, as they are, or certainly were in my early days, held in great abhorrence by the peasantry in the south of Ireland. One is a small brown lizard, which is occasionally found under stones; the other is a long, ugly-looking beetle, black and shining, with a forceps in his tail, which, when he is disturbed, he turns up over his back. A remarkably disagreeable-looking beast he is. The belief was that the little lizard, or *ardlucher* (as they called it in Irish), if you happened to fall asleep in a field or a wood, would watch its opportunity, slip into your mouth, and glide down into your inside, where it would feed and fatten till you pined away and died. I do not think they had any English name for the other beast, which they called a *darraghdeoul* (red devil). The tradition as to him was that he had, in some form or way, guided or accompanied Judas Iscariot to the garden of Gethsemane, the night of our Lord's betrayal. I have often seen a country boy kill one of them. The way he did it was always the same; he held it on the thumb-nail of his left hand and crushed it with the thumb-nail of his right hand. He believed that if he killed it so, saying at the same time a "Pater" or an "Ave," he was forgiven seven deadly sins; but unless the execution was carried out in strict conformity with the established rules no good result followed.

In some places pilgrimages are still made to holy lakes and wells of well-known healing virtues; and although the fairy doctors of whom I have spoken are now almost unknown, there still prevail, or lately did prevail, some peculiar ways of curing sickness. Amongst them were two modes of dealing with the whooping-cough, or "chin cough," as the peasantry call it. One is this: if any one should happen to pass by riding a piebald horse the father or mother of the whooper runs after him, crying out, " You that rides the piebald horse, what's good for the chin cough?" Whatever the rider prescribes, no matter how absurd, is procured and administered to the patient. This remedy, though the surest in its results, cannot always be secured, as it requires the presence of a piebald horse, and a man riding it. The other, though not quite so much to be depended on, is always at hand. It is to pass the child three times over and under a donkey, certain prayers being said during the operation. But there are donkeys and donkeys. Some are all but useless, while others are nearly as good as the piebald horse. I remember one, forty years ago, in Cork, famous for his powers. He was the property of one Ned Sullivan, who supported himself and a large family on what this remarkable donkey earned for him. Ned wandered through the city and surrounding country day after day with his ass, crying out, "Will any one come under my ass for the chin cough?"

Illnesses are also treated by remedies of comparatively recent date. Some five and forty years ago a temperance medal was found to be a specific for every ailment; not all medals, however, but only those which had been blest and given by Father Mathew, the great apostle of temperance. Rubbing with one of these at once relieved rheumatic pains. I have known one to be tied on the back of a man's hand to cure a boil, and I have seen ophthalmia treated by hanging two of these medals over a girl's eyes.

More recently still, Knock Chapel, in the county of Mayo, has been famous for its healing powers; but it, like the doctor, sometimes has its failures. Of one of these I was told by a Roman Catholic gentleman, my friend Mr. D——, a large employer of labour. One of his overseers had for years suffered much from his liver. Having consulted many doctors and spent much money on them, and being nothing better, he asked his employer to allow him to go for a few days to Knock to try what it could do for him. On his return Mr. D—— said to him—

"Well, James, I hope you are better?"

James. "Indeed, I'm no better, thank you, sir; it's what I think I'm rather worse."

Mr. D. "But did you go through all the forms required there?"

James. "Indeed I did, sir, and took all the rounds and said all the prayers, but it was all of no use; not but what it's a grand place. It would astonish you to see all the sticks and crutches hanging up there, left behind by poor cripples that went home cured. It's my opinion, Mr. D——, that for rheumatism and the like of that it's a grand place entirely; but as for the liver, it's not worth a d——."

Some men are sceptical about the power of medals and of Knock as others are as to that of doctors. Of the latter, was a peasant lad, who, when asked by a gentleman how his father was, replied—

"Ah, my poor father died last Wednesday, your honour."

"I'm sorry indeed to hear it," said the other. "It must have been very sudden. What doctor attended him?"

"Ah, sir," said the boy, "my poor father wouldn't have a doctor; he always used to say he'd like to die a natural death."

Of such, too, was my friend B——, who was one of a committee of subscribers to a fund for a monument to be erected in Mount Jerome Cemetery to the memory of a celebrated Dublin physician. A discussion arose as to the inscription. My friend recommended that it should be the same as that to Sir Christopher Wren in St. Paul's—"Si monumentum requiris circumspice."

Doctor Nedley, physician to the Dublin Metropolitan Police, told me he heard a voice from the crowd call out, "Three cheers for Doctor Nedley! He killed more policemen than ever the Fenians did!"

But if some men are sceptical, others place an implicit faith in the doctor's prescriptions; and of these was a man in Limerick who went to the undertaker to order a coffin for Pat Connell.

"Dear me," said the undertaker, "is poor Pat dead?"

"No, he's not dead yet," answered the other; "but he'll die to-night, for the doctor says he can't live till morning, and he knows what he gave him."

CHAPTER IX.

Mitchelstown remembered—A night on the Galtees—The weird horse—Killing or murder?—The ballad of "Shamus O'Brien"—A letter from Samuel Lover.

In a very hot July five and fifty years ago, a walking party left my father's house to visit some places of note in the counties of Limerick, Cork, and Tipperary. Our party consisted of John Walsh, afterwards Master of the Rolls in Ireland; John Jellett, the late Provost of Trinity College, Dublin; Gaetano Egedi, an Italian friend of ours; my brother, and myself. The weather being unusually warm, our plan was to start each day late in the afternoon, arriving at our destination about midnight, and visiting next day whatever was of interest in the neighbourhood. Towards the end of our tour we arrived late one night at Mitchelstown, famous for its caves, and now also of sacred political memory. Next morning we set off, immediately after breakfast, for the caves, which are about six miles from the town, near the village of Ballyporeen, celebrated in the old Irish song, "The Wedding of Ballyporeen," in which the wedding feast is thus described—

"There was bacon and greens, but the turkey was spoiled;
Potatoes dressed every way, roasted and boiled;
Red herrings, plum-pudding—the priest got a snipe;
Cobladdy, stiff dumpling, and cow-heel and tripe.
  Oh! they ate till they could ate no more, sir;
  Then the whisky came pouring galore, sir.
  How Terence McManus did roar, sir,
    At the wedding of Ballyporeen!"

The caves are in the cavernous limestone formation, and not unlike those of Derbyshire. We entered by a sort of ladder, which, after a descent of about thirty feet, leads to a long and narrow sloping passage, ending in a chamber about eighty feet in diameter, and thirty feet high. From this lofty hall a series of passages lead to other chambers of various sizes and heights; in many of them the stalactites from the roof uniting with the stalagmites from the floor form white pillars of glistening brightness; the whole effect of these halls when lighted up is very beautiful.

Having spent most of the day in the caves, we started about seven in the afternoon for Tipperary, which we hoped to reach by midnight. To go there by road would have been a walk of some five and twenty or thirty miles, while straight across the Galtee mountains was little more than half the distance; we therefore adopted the latter route. Lest we should lose our way, we secured the services of a guide, a fine young peasant, who said he knew the way across the mountains well. He could speak but little English; this however did not matter much, as we only wanted him to lead us. Off we set on this splendid summer evening, bright and calm. After a while we sat down for a little rest among the heather, high up on Galtee More. It was a glorious sight as we looked back on the great plain below us, with its green pastures and waving cornfields bathed in the light of the setting sun. We could not rest long, and were soon on foot again, and had nearly reached the crest of the range, when suddenly a fog rolled down upon us, so thick that we could not see more than thirty or forty yards. On we trudged, vainly hoping that the fog would lift; but, far from doing so, it grew darker every hour. We wandered on till we had crossed the summit; but soon after we and our guide had completely lost our way. On reaching the edge of a lake we asked the guide in which direction we should go round it, and found, as we had suspected, that he was as hopelessly lost as we were, and saw plainly that he had never known that there was a lake there. We went round by its margin till we came to a small stream flowing from it; we followed its course, knowing that it must lead us to the lower lands.

It was night now, and though the fog was as thick as ever, it was not altogether dark, as some little moonlight shone through it. The guide tried to cheer us up by constantly saying, "Nabochlish" (never mind), "the houses is near, the houses is near." Once, some fifteen or twenty yards from us, a horse galloped past; as well as we could see he was of a chestnut colour. We were too anxious to find our way to think much of this; but our guide brightened up immensely. "See the *coppel*" (the horse), "gentlemen," he said; "I tell'd ye the houses is near." But, alas! near the houses were not, and we had yet before us many a scramble through brakes of gorse, and many a tumble over rocks and tussocks. By this time the moon had gone down, and we were in complete darkness. The fog lifted as suddenly as it had come upon us. I forget which of us suggested that we should all shout together as loudly as we could, and thus, perhaps, attract the notice of some dweller on the slope of the mountain. After several shouts, to our joy, we heard in the distance an answering shout, and soon saw a bright light in the direction from which the welcome sounds had come. Shout answered shout as we hurried down; at times the light went out, but soon blazed up again.

At last, on the opposite side of a narrow glen full of rocks and brushwood, we saw the figures of men and women lighted up by a flaming sheaf of straw, which one of the men held up high in his hands. We quickly crossed the glen, and were at once surrounded. "Who are ye?" "What do ye want?" "Are ye peelers?" "What sort of gentlemen are ye at all to be on the mountains this time of night?" To these and many such-like questions we gave the best answers we could.

After a brief conversation, in Irish, with our guide, they led us to a large thatched farm-house; the habitation highest on the hills. They explained to us that they and some of their neighbours had been at the fair at Bansha and stayed out late, and just as they got home had heard our shouts. A huge turf fire was blazing on the hearth, at which we sat drying our nether garments, which were thoroughly drenched; great mugs of hot goat's milk were supplied to warm our insides, our host informing us that he had upwards of eighty goats on the mountain. He and the boys (all unmarried men are boys in the south) and girls sat up with us by the cheery fire, talking, joking, and telling stories. After some time my brother happened to say to the man of the house, " I suppose that was your horse that passed us on the mountain?"

All were silent, and looked one at another half incredulous, half frightened. One of them, after a pause, said, "There is no horse on the mountain. What sort of a horse was it that ye thought ye seen?"

" A chestnut horse," said we.

" Oh, begorra!" said our friend; " they seen the yalla horse!" Then turning to us, " It's a wonder ye all cum down alive and safe; it is few that sees the yalla horse that has luck after."

This was one of the superstitions of the dwellers on the Galtees. We afterwards thought that it might have been a red deer that passed us, as at that time it was supposed that there were a few of them, wild ones, still on the mountain. From what our entertainers told us it appears that had not the night been so calm, we should have been in considerable danger of an attack by the enchanted "wurrum," who had his abode in the dark lake we had passed; but fortunately for us it is only on wild and stormy nights that, with fearful roars, he emerges from the lake to waylay benighted wanderers.

One of the boys now asked us whether we had heard what had happened that day. As we had not, he told us that "a very responsible man," as he called him, had been shot dead that morning hard by towards Bansha. (He was, I think, Mr. Massey Dawson's steward or forester.) He did not exactly know, he said, why the man had been shot, but thought he was hard on the people about the price of timber, and had also dismissed some labourers.

Another of the boys said, "Now, why didn't they give him a good batin', and not to go kill him entirely?"

"Ah, then, I suppose," said the other, "they kem from a distance and didn't like to go home without finishing the job."

"But," said the other very seriously, "what will them chaps do on the day of judgment?"

"Oich," said his friend, "what does that signify? sure many a boy done a foolish turn."

It is not improbable that our friends knew perfectly well who had been engaged in the murder.

However that may be, early next morning we bid our entertainers a hearty farewell, and, again refreshed with hot goat's milk, started for the town of Tipperary, passing through the glen of Aherlow, then one of the most disturbed places in Ireland, about which the saying amongst the people was, "Wherever the devil is by day he is sure to be in the glen of Aherlow by night." It was the only time my brother saw that lovely valley, which he made the home of Shamus O'Brien in the popular ballad which I give here, as I do not think a correct version of it can elsewhere be found.

"SHAMUS O'BRIEN.

"Just after the war, in the year ninety-eight,
  As soon as the boys were all scattered and bate,
'Twas the custom, whenever a peasant was caught,
  To hang him by trial, barring such as was shot.
There was trial by jury goin' on by daylight,
  And the martial law hangin' the lavings by night.
It's them was hard times for an honest gossoon:
  If he missed in the judges, he'd meet a dragoon;
And whether the judge or the soldiers gave sentence,
  The divil a much time they allowed for repentance.
And it's many's the fine boy was then on his keeping,
  With small share of restin', or atin', or sleepin',
And because they loved Erin, and scorned to sell it,
  A prey for the bloodhound, a mark for the bullet,
Unsheltered by night, and unrested by day,
  With the heath for their barrack, revenge for their pay.
And the bravest and hardiest boy of them all
  Was Shamus O'Brien, from the town of Glengall.
His limbs were well set, and his body was light,
  And the keen fangéd hound hadn't teeth half so white;

But his face was as pale as the face of the dead,
And his cheek never warmed with the blush of the red;
And for all that he wasn't an ugly young boy,
For the divil himself couldn't blaze with his eye,
So funny and so wicked, so dark and so bright,
Like the fire-flash that crosses the depth of the night.
And he was the best mower that ever has been,
And the illigantest hurler that ever was seen;
In fincin' he gave Patrick Mooney a cut,
And in jumpin' he bate Tim Maloney a foot.
For lightness of foot there wasn't his peer,
For, begorra, you'd think he'd outrun the red deer;
And his dancin' was such that the men used to stare,
And the women turned crazy, he had done it so quare—
And, begorra, the whole world gave in to him there.
And it's he was the boy that was hard to be caught,
And it's often he ran, and it's often he fought,
And it's many's the one can remember right well
The quare things he done; and it's often I heerd tell
How he frightened the magistrate in Cahirbally,
And escaped through the soldiers in Aherlow Valley,
And leathered the yeomen himself agin' four,
And stretched the two strongest on old Galtimore.
But the fox must sleep sometimes, the wild deer must rest,
And treachery preys on the blood of the best.
After many a brave action of power and pride,
And many a hard night on the mountain's bleak side,
And a thousand great dangers and toils overpast,
In the darkness of night he was taken at last.

"Now, Shamus, look back on the beautiful moon,
For the door of the prison must close on you soon;
And take your last look at her dim lovely light,
That falls on the mountain and valley this night;
One look at the village, one look at the flood,
And one at the sheltering, far-distant wood.
Farewell to the forest, farewell to the hill,
And farewell to the friends that will think of you still;
Farewell to the hurlin', the pattern, and wake,
And farewell to the girl that would die for your sake.

"Well, twelve soldiers brought him to Maryboro' jail,
And the turnkey received him, refusin' all bail;
The fleet limbs were chained, and the strong hands were
    bound,
And he laid down his length on the cold prison ground.
And the dreams of his childhood came over him there,
As gentle and soft as the sweet summer air;
And happy remembrances crowding on ever,
As fast as the foam-flakes drift down the river,
Bringing fresh to his heart merry days long gone by,
Till the tears gathered heavy and thick in his eye.
But the tears didn't fall, for the pride of his heart
Wouldn't suffer one drop down his pale cheek to start;
And he sprang to his feet in the dark prison cave,
And he swore with the fierceness that misery gave,
By the hopes of the good, by the cause of the brave,
That when he was mouldering in his cold grave
His enemies never should have it to boast
His scorn of their vengeance one moment was lost;
His bosom might bleed, but his cheek should be dry,
For undaunted he'd lived, and undaunted he'd die.

"Well, as soon as a few weeks were over and gone,
The terrible day of the trial came on.
There was such a crowd there was scarce room to stand,
With soldiers on guard, and dragoons sword in hand;
And the court-house so full that the people was bothered,
And attorneys and criers on the point of being smothered;
And counsellors almost given over for dead,
And the jury sittin' up in their box overhead;
And the judge settled out, so determined and big,
With his gown on his back, and an illigant new wig.
And silence was called, and the minute it was said,
The court was as still as the heart of the dead,
And they heard but the opening of one prison lock,
And Shamus O'Brien came into the dock.
For one minute he turned his eye round on the throng,
And he looked on the bars, so firm and so strong,
And he saw that he hadn't a hope nor a friend,
A chance to escape nor a word to defend;

And he folded his arms as he stood there alone,
As calm and as cold as a statue of stone.
And they read a big writin', a yard long at laste,
And Jim didn't understand it or mind it a taste.
And the judge took a big pinch of snuff, and he says,
'Are you guilty or not, Jim O'Brien, if you plase?'
And they all held their breath in the silence of dread;
And Shamus O'Brien made answer and said,
'My lord, if you ask me if in my life-time
I thought any treason or done any crime
That should call to my cheek, as I stand alone here,
The hot blush of shame or the coldness of fear,
Though I stood by the grave to receive my death-blow,
Before God and the world I answer you, "No!"
But if you would ask me, as I think it like,
If in the rebellion I carried a pike,
And fought for old Ireland from the first to the close,
And shed the heart's blood of her bitterest foes,
I answer you, "Yes!" and I tell you again,
Though I stand here to perish, it's my glory that then
In her cause I was willing my veins should run dry,
And that now for her sake I am ready to die.'
Then the silence was great, and the jury smiled bright,
And the judge wasn't sorry the job was made light;
By my sowl! it's himself was the crabbed old chap,
In a twinklin' he pulled on his ugly black cap.

"Then Shamus's mother, in the crowd standing by,
Called out to the judge with a pitiful cry:
'Oh, judge darlin', don't!—oh, don't say the word!
The crathur is young; have mercy, my lord!
He was foolish, he didn't know what he was doin';
You don't know him, my lord—oh, don't give him to ruin!
He's the kindliest crathur, the tenderest hearted,
Don't part us for ever, we that's so long parted!
Judge, mavourneen, forgive him! forgive him, my lord!
And God will forgive you. Oh, don't say the word?'

"That was the first minute that O'Brien was shaken,
When he saw that he wasn't quite forgot or forsaken;

And down his pale cheeks, at the words of his mother,
The big tears were runnin' fast, one after th' other;
And he tried hard to hide them or wipe them away,
But in vain, for his hands were too fast bound that day.
And two or three times he endeavoured to spake,
But the strong, manly voice used to falter and break;
Till at last, by the strength of his high-mounting pride,
He conquered and mastered his grief's swelling tide.
And says he, 'Mother darlin', don't break your poor heart,
For sooner or later the dearest must part.
And God knows it's better than wandering in fear
On the bleak, trackless mountain among the wild deer,
To lie in the grave, where the head, hand, and breast
From thought, labour, and sorrow for ever shall rest.
Then, mother, my darlin', don't cry any more,
Don't make me seem broken in this my last hour;
For I wish, when my head is lyin' under the raven,
No true man can say that I died like a craven!'
Then towards the judge Shamus bowed down his head,
And that minute the solemn death sentence was said.

"The morning was bright, and the mist rose on high,
And the lark whistled merrily in the clear sky.
But why are the men standin' idle so late?
And why do the crowds gather fast in the street?
What come they to talk of? what come they to see?
And why does the long rope hang from the cross-tree?
Now, Shamus O'Brien, pray fervent and fast;
May the saints take your soul! for this day is your last;
Pray fast, and pray strong, for the moment is nigh
When, strong, proud, and great as you are, you must die.
And faster and faster the crowd gathered there—
Boys, horses, and gingerbread, just like a fair;
And whisky was sellin', and cussamuck too,
And ould men and young women enjoyin' the view;
And ould Tim Mulvany he made the remark,
'There wasn't such a sight since the time of Noah's ark.'
And, begorra, 'twas true for him, the divil such a scruge,
Such divarshin and crowds was known since the deluge!
Ten thousand was gathered there, if there was one,
All waitin' till such time as the hangin' 'id come on.

"SHAMUS O'BRIEN."

At last they threw open the big prison gate,
And out come the sheriffs and soldiers in state,
And a cart in the middle, and Shamus was in it,
Not paler, but prouder than ever that minute.
And as soon as the people saw Shamus O'Brien,
With prayin' and blessin' and all the girls cryin',
A wild, wailin' sound came on by degrees,
Like the sound of the lonesome wind blowin' through trees.
On, on to the gallows the sheriffs are gone,
And the cart and the soldiers go steadily on;
And at every side swellin' around of the cart,
A wild, sorrowful sound that would open your heart.
Now under the gallows the cart takes its stand,
And the hangman gets up with the rope in his hand;
And the priest gives his blessing and goes down on the ground,
And Shamus O'Brien throws one last look round.
Then the hangman drew near, and the people grew still,
Young faces turned sickly and warm hearts grew chill.
And all being ready, his neck was made bare
For the gripe of the life-stranglin' cord to prepare;
And the good priest has left him, having said his last prayer.
But the good priest done more, for his hands he unbound,
And with one daring spring Jim has leaped on the ground!
Bang! bang! go the carbines, and clash go the sabres!
' He's not down! he's alive still! now stand to him, neighbours!
Through the smoke and the horses, he's into the crowd!
By the heavens he is free!' than thunder more loud,
By one shout from the people the heavens were shaken—
One shout that the dead of the world might awaken.
Your swords they may glitter, your carbines go bang,
But if you want hangin', it's yourselves you must hang,
For to-night he'll be sleepin' in Aherlow glen,
And the divil's in the dice if you catch him again.
The soldiers ran this way, the hangman ran that,
And Father Malone lost his new Sunday hat;
And the sheriffs were both of them punished severely,
And fined like the divil because Jim done them fairly."

The ballad was written in a very few days, in the year 1840, and sent to me day by day by my brother as he wrote it to Dundalk, where I was then staying. I quickly learned it by heart, and now and then recited it. The scraps of paper on which it was written were lost, and years after, when my brother wished for a copy, I had to write it out from memory for him. One other copy I wrote out in the same way and gave to Samuel Lover when he was starting on his tour through the United States, where, as will be seen by the following letter, it was received with much applause:—

"Astor House, New York, U.S., America,
"September 30, 1846.

"MY DEAR LE FANU,

"In reading over your brother's poem while I crossed the Atlantic, I became more and more impressed with its great beauty and dramatic effect; so much so that I determined to test its effect in public, and have done so here, on my first appearance, with the greatest success. Now I have no doubt there will be great praises of the poem, and people will suppose most likely that the composition is mine, and, as you know (I take it for granted) that I would not wish to wear a borrowed feather, I should be glad to give your brother's name as author, should he not object to have it known; but as his writings are often of so different a tone, I would not speak without permission to do so. It is true that in my programme my name is attached to the other pieces, and no name appended to the recitation; so far you will see I have done all I could to avoid 'appropriating,' the spirit of which I might have caught here with Irish aptitude; but I would like to have the means of telling all whom it may concern the name of the author to whose head and heart it does so much honour. Pray, my dear Le Fanu, inquire and answer me here by next packet, or as soon as convenient. My success here has been quite triumphant.

"Yours very truly,
"SAMUEL LOVER."

Notwithstanding his disclaimer of authorship, I afterwards, more than once, heard the poem attributed to Lover. He did, indeed, add a few lines, by no means an improvement to it, in which he makes Shamus emigrate to America, where he sets up a public-house, and writes home to his mother to invite her to come out and live with him in his happy home. I suppose he thought that this would suit the taste of the Irish-Americans.

Many years after this, when I had recited the poem at the house of my friend, Sir William Stirling Maxwell, he said, "I was afraid poor Shamus would be hanged." "I didn't think so for a moment," said Lord Dufferin. "Why?" said Sir William. "Possibly," said Lord Dufferin, "it may have been because I have heard William Le Fanu recite it once or twice before."

There are a few words and phrases in "Shamus O'Brien" which some of my readers may not understand. I give them here with their meaning.

"Just after the war." The peasants always call the rebellion of 1798 "the War."

"On his keeping," in hiding from the police or soldiers.

"The illigantest hurler." "Hurling" (or "hurley," as it is now called) was formerly the chief game in Ireland.

"Gossoon," or "gorsoon," a young lad.

"Pattern," a gathering for religious purposes or for cures at a holy well, or some other place, dedicated to some patron saint. The word is a corruption of "patron."

K

CHAPTER X.

A determined duel—I act the peasant, and am selected for the police force—Death of my sister—Sketch of my brother's life—Dan O'Connell's "illustrious kinsman"—A murderous Grand Jury—A sad reflection.

It was just about the year 1838 that a duel—one of the last, if not the last, in this country—was fought, of which a Mr. Ireland, then at the Irish Bar, gave me the following account :—

The cause of the quarrel was some joke which a Mr. O'Hara had made at the expense of a Mr. Robert Napoleon Finn, who at once challenged him to mortal combat. O'Hara, like a brave Galway man as he was, refused to make the slightest apology, and preliminaries were quickly settled by the seconds. It was arranged that the meeting should take place at five a.m. next morning, on the sands at the North Bull, a lonely place at the seaside, about three miles from Dublin. Ireland, who was a friend of both the principals, was invited to accompany the party as *amicus curiæ*. Next morning, when they arrived on the ground, they took off their greatcoats, and laid them in a pile on the sand, and on them Ireland took his seat.

It was arranged that one of the seconds, who had had some little previous experience in affairs of honour, should give the signal for the combatants to fire. When they were in their places, twelve paces apart, this second, standing between them, proceeded to give them instructions as to how the fight was to be conducted. "The only signal will be," he said, "the words, 'Ready—fire.'" At the word "fire," Finn, in his nervous excitement, raised his pistol, pointing it towards the second. "Be quiet, will you?" said he. "Do you want to shoot me?" Having retired a few paces to be out of danger, he went on to say, "Neither of you is to attempt to raise your pistol till I give the word 'ready,' nor to attempt to shoot till I give the word 'fire.'" At the word "fire" Finn again lost his head, pulled the trigger of his pistol, which was pointed downwards, and lodged the bullet in the calf of his own leg. O'Hara, thinking that Finn had taken a shot at him, immediately took aim at him, while Finn hopped off as fast as his wounded leg would let him, crying out, "For God's sake, don't fire; it was all a mistake!" But O'Hara did fire, and his bullet struck the ground close to Finn, and sent the sand flying over Ireland and the coats. At that moment four constables appeared on the ground with warrants for the arrest of the whole party, who were quickly captured, placed in the carriages in which they had come, and driven back to Dublin, Finn's leg the while dangling out of the carriage window to keep it cool. The affair caused much amusement in Dublin, and it was said, I think, by Pat Costello, that "Finn had gone to the Bull, got cow'd, and shot the calf."

After 1839 I was comparatively little at Abington. I had in that year become one of the pupils of Sir John MacNeill, the well-known civil engineer. About a year after I had joined his staff I had gone to a fancy ball in the south of Ireland as an Irish peasant—frieze coat, corduroy knee-breeches, yellow waistcoat, grey stockings, and brogues; in my fist a good blackthorn, and on my head a wig, with the hair cropped quite close, except the national glib, or forelock, then the fashion amongst the southern peasantry. When I came back to Dublin, I went to MacNeill's office dressed in the same way, and so perfect was the disguise that I completely took him in, as well as my fellow-pupils. I told them I had come all the way from Clonmel to look for work, and couldn't find any, and wanted to get home again, but hadn't the means; and then and there they made a subscription to enable me to get back to my native Tipperary.

Amongst the pupils was Hemans, son of Mrs. Hemans the poetess, afterwards highly distinguished in his profession. He then lived in Dublin Castle, at the official residence of his uncle, Colonel Browne, Chief Commissioner of Police, with whom I often dined and spent my evenings. Hemans was so much pleased with the trick I had played that he insisted on my going to the Castle, disguised in the same way, to apply to his uncle for an appointment as constable in the Dublin Metropolitan Police. So I wrote a letter to Colonel Browne in my own name, saying that the bearer, Pat Ryan, was a most respectable young man, one of my father's parishioners, who was very anxious to be a policeman, and that I should be very much obliged if he could appoint him. With this letter in my pocket, I took a covered car (there were no cabs in Dublin then), and drove to the police office in the Castle. I told the driver to wait for me, and was ushered by a policeman into a large hall, where were assembled several candidates for admission into the force, and also some constables. On entering I looked about, and said—

"Gentlemen, which of yez is Colonel Browne, if ye plaze?"

A policeman came up to me, and said, "Colonel Browne is not in the room. What is it you want?"

"Well, sir," said I, "it's a bit of a writin' I have that Mr. Le Fanu gave me for the Colonel."

"Give it to me," said he, "and I'll give it to him."

"Not by no manner of means," said I; "for Mr. Le Fanu towld me not to give it to any one, only into the Colonel's own hands; and, begorra, I'd be affeared to give it to any one else, so I must see him myself."

The policeman replied, "If you don't give me the letter you won't see him at all. Don't be afraid; I'll give it to him safe enough."

"Under them circumstances, sir," said I, "I'll trust you with it; but, my good man, you must give it to the Colonel at once, for Mr. Le Fanu will be displeased if I'm kept waitin'."

I was, however, kept a long time, during which I had a good deal of talk with other candidates. Amongst them was a very dapper little fellow, neatly dressed, but plainly quite too small and slight for the police. He looked rather contemptuously at my get-up, and said—

"Now, do you think you have much chance of being appointed?"

"Well, my tight fellow," said I, "if we are to judge by personal appearance and shapes, I think I have as good a chance as you, any way."

He retired, and a friendly constable came up to me, and said, " What part of the country do you come from?"

"I'm from Tipperary," said I.

"I thought so," said he; "I partly guessed I knew the frieze. And in what part of Tipperary do you live?"

"Not very far from Newport," said I.

"Oh, then," said he, "I suppose you know the Doodeys?"

"Of coorse I do," said I. "Why wouldn't I know them?" (I had never heard of them.)

"And how is old Mick Doodey?" said he.

"He's illigant," said I.

"And how is little Tom?" he asked.

"He's illigant too," said I, "only in regard of a sort of a swelling he has in his jaw."

"He was always subject to that," said he; then, looking at my hair, which was too long, and was coming out below the wig at the back of my head, he said, "What makes your hair so long at the back?"

"I suppose," said I, "when my hair was shaved off last Candlemas, when I had the sickness, that the front and the back of it grew longer since than the other parts."

"Come in with me for a minute," said he, "and I'll crop it off for you in the way you'll look neat and tidy when you're called up."

"I thank you kindly," said I, "but I'll not mind it just now; it will be time enough to crop it if I'm appointed."

"Well, anyhow," said he, "hould up your head, and don't look any way afeared or daunted like when you go up before the Colonel."

Our conversation was then interrupted, as I was ordered upstairs to appear before the Colonel. As I entered his room I took off my hat and my brogues, and laid them with my blackthorn on the floor beside me. There was my old friend seated at his desk in all the dignity of office. After he had taken a good long look at me, he said—

"It was you, I think, who brought me this letter from Mr. Le Fanu?"

"It was, my lord."

" You want to go into the police?"

" That's my ambition, your raverence."

" Can you read and write?"

" Why not,'your worship? Sure I got a nate edication."

" Well, read that," said he, handing me a letter, which I begun to read as follows :—" Sir, I am anxious to become a member of the M-E *me*, T-R-O *tro*, P-O *po*—— Ah, begorra, my lord," said I, " that long word bates me!"

" Never mind," he said; " it is ' metropolitan.' Go on."

I got through the rest of the letter swimmingly.

" Take him down now," said he, " and have him measured, and then bring him back here."

I was taken down and put under the measuring instrument, where I kept bobbing up my head to make myself taller.

" Keep quiet, will you?" said the sergeant, putting his hand on my head. "You have a wig on?"

" Of course I have," said I.

" Remove it at once," said he.

" No, nor the dickens a taste," said I. " Didn't ye hear the Colonel tellin' me not to dar to take off that wig be reason of a cowld I have in my head?"

So I was measured with my wig on, due allowances being, no doubt, made for it, and was marched up to the Colonel again.

" Exactly six foot, sir," said the sergeant.

The Colonel then said to me, " You are to attend

here on Friday morning next, at ten o'clock, to be examined by the doctor; and you may tell Mr. Le Fanu that if you pass the doctor I intend to put you into the B division."

"Long may your honour live!" said I; then, handing him one of my visiting cards, I added, "Mr. Le Fanu bid me give you that."

"Where is Mr. Le Fanu?" said he.

"Here, your raverence," said I.

"What do you mean?" he asked me.

"Ah, then, Colonel dear, you ould villain, look at me now. Is it because I'm in these plain clothes you purtind not to know me?"

Up he jumped, put his arm in mine, and for some minutes laughed so heartily that he could not say a word, while the sergeant and the orderly stood near the door, in amazement, thinking we had both gone off our heads. As soon as he could speak he said, "Come to dine at half-past seven, and we'll talk about the B division."

I ran downstairs to the hall, where candidates came about me, asking, "Are you appointed?"

"Appointed, ye blackguards of the world!" said I. "Appointed, is it! I'm not only appointed, but, begorra, I'm to dine with the Colonel."

I then ran out, got into my car, and drove off. I did not come back on Friday to the doctor; but many years afterwards I got a good appointment on the Great Southern Railway for Barrett, the constable who had been so good to me.

In the spring of 1841 a great grief befell us in the death of our only sister, the constant and loved companion of our young days. Her cleverness, her sweet temper, and, above all, her wondrous goodness, had endeared her, not to us alone, but to all who knew her. Without a particle of that cant or one of those shibboleths which spoil the conversation and mar the usefulness of so many, she influenced for good all who came in contact with her. She was the idol of the poor in our neighbourhood. There are still old people at Abington who speak of her as "the good Miss Catherine," and tell of all the good she did.

She had been early a contributor to the *Dublin University Magazine*, in which she wrote most pleasantly, but fell into ill-health and died when she was twenty-seven. She was her father's darling. After her death he never was the same, and did not very long survive her. We were summoned from Dublin to her death-bed. Great was her joy at seeing us and having us with her. She had feared that we would not arrive in time to see her.

It was in this same year, 1841, that my brother took his B.A. degree in the University, and soon afterwards was called to the Irish Bar. But he almost immediately became connected with the Press, and proprietor and editor of the *Warder*, a paper of note in Ireland; and shortly afterwards he purchased another paper, which he also edited. This was injurious to his future prospects, as it prevented his applying himself to a profession, for which his eloquence and ready wit fitted him, and of which his contemporaries had hoped to see him a distinguished member. Later on he purchased, and for some time edited, the *Dublin University Magazine*. It was in that periodical he published the first of Rhoda Broughton's novels. She was first cousin to my brother's wife, Susan Bennett, the charming daughter of the late George Bennett, Q.C., whom he married in the year 1844.

In 1845 the first and one of his best novels, "The Cock and Anchor, a Chronicle of old Dublin City," appeared; and very soon his second, "The Fortunes of Turloch O'Brien." They were published in Dublin, and were unsuccessful. I know not why, for they were quite equal to some of his most successful novels.

Owing to their want of success, and to the amount of time he was obliged to devote to the Press, he did not for eighteen years again take up his pen as a novelist. It was not until 1863 that his next story, "The House by the Churchyard," appeared. It was soon followed by "Uncle Silas," the best known of his novels, and afterwards by five others.

His wife, to whom he was devotedly attached, died in 1858, and from this time he entirely forsook general society, and was seldom seen except by his near relations and a few familiar friends. In the year 1871, almost immediately after the publication of his last novel, "Willing to Die," he breathed his last in his house in Merrion Square. One who knew him long and well thus speaks of him in a short memoir which appeared, in the *University Magazine,* soon after his death: "He was a man who thought deeply, especially on religious subjects. To those who knew him he was very dear. They admired him for his learning, his sparkling wit, and pleasant conversation, and loved him for his manly virtues, for his noble and generous qualities, his gentleness, and his loving, affectionate nature."

All who knew my brother will feel the truth of these few simple words.

As MacNeill had an office in London, as well as one in Dublin, I had to be a good deal there during my pupilage, and for twenty years afterwards I spent a good part of every spring and early summer there—first as MacNeill's assistant, and subsequently to attend before Parliamentary committees to give evidence on bills for railways and other works, of which I was engineer.

In those days, amongst Irishmen resident in London, was a well-known character, called amongst his friends "Lord Kilmallock," or, more generally, "Kilmallock," owing to his having been born in the little town of that name in the county of Limerick, whence he emigrated to the big city. His real name was O'Connell. Though no relation of the famous Dan O'Connell, he wished to be thought so, and on every occasion took up the cudgels for his "illustrious kinsman," as he always called him. Of him the "Liberator's" nephew, Morgan John O'Connell, the M.P. (for Kerry, I think), told me many anecdotes, amongst them the following:—

O'Connell, in one of his violent speeches, told his audience that Disraeli was a lineal descendant of the impenitent thief. Disraeli at once challenged him; but O'Connell refused to meet him, having registered a vow that he would never fight again, owing to his having killed Mr. D'Esterre in a duel in the early days of his career. Kilmallock considered it his duty at once to take up the quarrel, and wrote to Disraeli to the following effect:—

> "Sir,—I understand that you have sent a challenge to my illustrious kinsman, the great Daniel O'Connell, well knowing that owing to a solemn vow he could not meet you; but I, sir, as his relative, and endorsing every word he said of you, am prepared to give you that satisfaction which one gentleman owes to another, and am ready to meet you at any time and place you name—here, in France, in Germany, or even at the foot of that mount where your impenitent ancestor suffered for his crimes."

About the same time an English member of Parliament, Mr. Chambers, brought forward every Session a motion in the House of Commons, with a view of having a Government inspection of nunneries. A friend called on Kilmallock the morning after a debate on one of these motions. He found him very busy writing.

"What are you writing about, Kilmallock?" he asked.

"I'm writing a letter to the editor of the *Times* about that scoundrel Chambers. I'll read you as much as I have written :—

"To the Editor of the *Times*.

"Sir,—I see by your paper of this date that last night in the House of Commons Mr. Chambers brought forward his usual motion in favour of Government inspection of Catholic nunneries. Instead of attacking those amiable, pious, virtuous ladies, the Catholics nuns, let this Mr. Chambers look nearer home; let him look at his own old card-playing, scandal-mongering, dram-drinking mother——"

"But," interrupted his friend, "take care that that is not libellous. Are you quite sure she is so bad?"

"What would I know about the old divil?" said Kilmallock. "I never heard of her in my life. But if he has a particle of manly feeling in his composition it will cut him to the quick."

Morgan John O'Connell, in introducing Kilmallock to a friend, said, "Allow me to introduce to you my namesake, Mr. O'Connell." "Your illustrious uncle," Kilmallock said, "would have said '*my kinsman*.'" "That is his vanity," said Morgan John.

It was Kilmallock, I think, who told me of a Grand Jury case which occurred many years before in his own county of Kerry.

At the spring assizes at Tralee the Grand Jury,

who had been considering a murder case, came from their room into court to consult the judge. The foreman said, "My lord, how can we find a bill for wilful murder when the murdered man himself is giving evidence before us?" "Quite impossible, gentlemen," said the judge. "But, my lord," said one of the jury, "as the man was nearly killed, couldn't we find a bill for manslaughter?" "Equally impossible, gentlemen," said the judge.

The way in which the matter arose was this: In the winter before, a farmer had been attacked and beaten almost to death about fifteen miles from Tralee. He was found on the road insensible, and carried into a cabin. The inmates did not know whether he was alive or dead, so to be right in either case they sent to Tralee for the doctor and the coroner, who both arrived in the afternoon in a storm of sleet and snow. On examining the injured man the doctor said he could not possibly recover or even live through the night. The coroner asked him whether it was absolutely certain that he would die before morning. The doctor replied, "Absolutely certain." "In that case," said the coroner, "I may as well hold my inquest on him, for he is dead to all intents and purposes, and what would be the use of my going back to Tralee only to come out here again to-morrow in this awful weather?" So a jury was brought together, who quickly found a verdict of "Wilful murder against some person or persons unknown." But in spite of doctor and coroner the man recovered, and thus was able to appear before the Grand Jury.

Another of Kilmallock's stories was of a young Irishman in mourning, on board one of the river boats, who, as it passed Greenwich, was seen to burst into tears and cover his face with his handkerchief. On being asked what was the cause of his emotion, "Look at that building," said he, pointing to Greenwich Hospital—"look at it! It reminds me of my dear father's stables in Connemara!"

CHAPTER XI.

The power of the people — Sergeant Murphy; his London manners — Pat Costello's humour — I meet Thackeray — Paddy Blake's echo — Dan O'Connell's imagination — Sir James O'Connell's anecdotes — He is prayed for by his herd.

AT one of Dan O'Connell's elections, during the Repeal agitation, where the speaking was pretty stormy, one of the speakers, a Mr. MacSheehey, exclaimed in stentorian tones, "We'll hurl the British lion from his pedestal!" A voice from the crowd was heard to cry, "Mr. MacSheehey! Mr. MacSheehey! if I was you I'd let that baste alone, or maybe you'll find his claws in your tail some fine morning."

This reminds me of a friend of mine, who at one time thought of contesting the borough of Tralee, his native town. In his maiden speech he used the words, "The power of the people, once roused, can hurl the mightiest potentate from his throne!" Next morning, in reading the report of his speech in the *Tralee Chronicle*, he found to his horror he was made to say, "The power of the people, once roused, can hurl the mightiest Hottentot from his throne." Whether it was owing to the fun

L

that was made of him about his speech or from some other cause I cannot say, but he never spoke in public again.

A misprint of something of the same kind occurred in the report of a speech of O'Connell's, in which he was made to say that "He would always stand up for religious liberty and for the right of every man to horsewhip his God after the dictates of his conscience." The report had changed "worship" into "horsewhip." Strange to say this misprint appeared in the paper which, at the time, was the strongest supporter of O'Connell.

Another Irishman well known in London then was Sergeant Murphy, generally known as "Frank Murphy." He was member of Parliament for Cork, his native city, and distinguished at the Bar and in the House of Commons. Pleasant and witty he was, considerably bumptious too. When he visited Cork during vacation, his great delight was to astonish the natives by his London ways and manners. At a large dinner-party at the house of an old gentleman, a relative and namesake of his, where many Murphys were assembled, immediately after dinner he lit a cigar and began to smoke, a custom unheard of in Ireland then. There was much astonishment amongst the guests. His old host, however, was equal to the occasion, and at once said, "Indeed, then, it is kind for you, Frank, for your old grandmother always took a shaugh of the pipe after the pratees."

In Murphy's time, Spooner and Newdegate were the two ultra-Protestant Tories in the House of Commons. Of these he said, "The degrees of comparison of the word 'spoon' are 'Spoon,' 'Spooner,' 'Newdegate.'"

He was a friend of Warren, author of "Ten Thousand a Year," a most conceited man. When this book was coming out in numbers in, I think, *Fraser's Magazine*, the two met at a large dinner-party in London, and, though the story was coming out anonymously, Murphy and most of the other guests knew perfectly well it was Warren's. After dinner, when the conversation was general, Warren, who was always fishing for compliments, said to Murphy across the table —

"Have you read that thing that is coming out in *Fraser*?"

"What thing?" said Murphy.

"'Ten Thousand a Year,'" said Warren.

"Yes, I have read it," he answered.

"What do you think of it?" asked Warren.

"Hardly fair to ask me," said Murphy, "for I wrote it."

I have heard a story told of Murphy, but which really happened to quite another man, a resident in Kerry, who dearly loved a lord, and lost no opportunity of talking of his great acquaintances. At a dinner-party where there were several Roman Catholics, during a conversation on the subject of fasting, this gentleman said, "It is very strange how little Catholics in the higher ranks mind the fast days. I was dining at the Duke of Norfolk's on a fast day, three weeks ago, and there wasn't a bit of fish at dinner." "I suppose," said Pat Costello, "they had eaten it all in the dining-room?"

This Pat Costello had been on very intimate terms with a fellow barrister, O'Loughlin, afterwards Sir Michael O'Loughlin and Master of the Rolls in Ireland. As "Pat" and "Michael" they were wont to address each other. Soon after the latter was appointed Master of the Rolls, he met Pat and said to him, "How do you do, Mr. Costello?" "Mr. Costello!" said Pat. "Bedad, you'd think it was I that was Master of the Rolls."

A friend who met him unexpectedly said, "Are you here, Pat? I heard you had gone up the Rhine with Billy Stephens." "Up the Rhine with Billy Stephens!" said Pat. "I wouldn't go up the Dodder with him." The Dodder is a little stream passing through the suburbs of Dublin into the Liffey.

It is told of him that, on a Friday at a mail-coach dinner, when there was only a small piece of salmon, all of which the only other Roman Catholic passenger was taking to himself, Pat interposed, and insisted on having half of it, saying, "Do you think, sir, no one has a soul to be saved but yourself?"

He was not of the same mind as the Roman Catholic gentleman who, when asked why he ate meat on Friday, said that fish always disagreed with him and gave him dyspepsia, and that though he had a

Catholic heart, he greatly feared he had a Protestant stomach.

On one of my visits to London, I found that my old friend Johnny Jones, a most amusing fellow, formerly one of Sir J. MacNeill's assistants, had become famous as a sculptor. My first acquaintance with Thackeray was through him, and came about on this wise. Jones came one night into my hotel and told me he had just come up from Greenwich, where he, Thackeray, and two or three others had been dining together.

"By-the-by," said he, "don't you know Thackeray?"

"I am sorry to say I do not," said I.

"Then," said he, "come and dine with me to-morrow and you'll meet him."

"Where do you dine?" I asked.

"At my friend Bevan's, in Coleman Street."

"But," I answered, "I do not know Mr. Bevan. I never even heard of him."

"That doesn't make the slightest difference," said Johnny. "He's the best fellow in the world—sings like a nightingale—and will be glad to see you."

"But," I objected, "how could I go to dine at the house of a man when I don't know him?"

Johnny replied, "If I ask you, it's exactly the same as if he asked you. He has given me a *carte blanche* to ask any one I choose; and I often bring a friend to dine with him. If you don't come we'll be only five to-morrow, and six would be pleasanter, and he would like it better. I'll tell you what sort of a man Bevan is. About three months ago he asked me to stay with him for a few days. I am with him still; and he is such a good fellow and such a pleasant fellow, I do not think I'll ever leave him."

So I accepted the invitation, and on my arrival at Coleman Street next day, found Mr. Bevan all that Johnny had described him. A pleasant little party we were; Bevan and Johnny at head and foot of the table, Hobhouse and Mozley at one side, Thackeray and I at the other, and with songs and stories we kept it up well into the small hours.

Thackeray was always pleasant when I afterwards met him; but so pleasant and in such spirits as he was that night I never saw him. I happened to mention an amusing dissertation which I had heard that morning between Lord Redesdale, Chairman of Committees of the Lords, and Venables, then one of the leading parliamentary agents. I asked Thackeray whether he knew Venables. "I ought to know him," said he; "it was he who broke my nose."

In telling an Irish story, few could equal Jones. He sang well, too; but in Irish songs, gay or plaintive, another Johnny far surpassed him. His was one of the sweetest and most touching voices I have ever heard. He was Johnny, eldest son of the late, and brother of the present Sir Thomas

Deane, the distinguished architect. Several years after the time I have been speaking of, these two were the life and soul of a large party who spent a few days at Killarney when Lord Carlisle, then Lord Lieutenant of Ireland, came down to open the railway there, of which I was engineer. Some of the party, amongst whom were Judge Haliburton (Sam Slick), Shirley Brooks, Johnny Jones, and myself, had been through the Gap of Dunloe and came down the lakes. It was a very windy day, so windy that though Spillane, our bugler, played his best at the Eagle's Nest and other points, no echo could we get. Again he tried at Glena; but all in vain. No answer came to the bugle sound; so we determined to try whether we could awake an echo by shouting all together at the top of our voices. We sang out, "Ho, ho, Johnny Jones!" A soft and gentle echo from the mountain answered, "Ho, ho, Johnny Deane!" Surely, thought we, we must have misheard. We called again, "Ho, ho, Johnny Jones!" More clearly than before the echo said, "Ho, ho, Johnny Deane!" Again and again we tried, but got no other reponse. "Begorra," said one of our boatmen, "often as I heard tell of Paddy Blake's echo, I never believed in it till now."

Paddy Blake's echo is well known at Killarney. When you call out, "How are you, Paddy Blake?" Echo answers, "Well, I thank you, sir." In the evening the mystery was solved. Johnny Deane himself was the echo. He and some others of our friends had climbed Glena and heard and answered our shouting from its wooded side.

When Lord Carlisle made a speech on the opening of the railway, there stood near me a reporter of one of the Kerry papers, who asked me the names of the people by whom his Excellency was attended. Amongst them was Walter Creyke, then in deacon's orders and chaplain to Lord Carlisle. "Who is the handsome young man with the dark beard?" said my neighbour. "Mr. Creyke," said I, "the Lord Lieutenant's chaplain." "Do you know his Christian name?" he said. "Corn," said I. In the morning's paper he duly appeared as "the Rev. Corn Creyke."

It was then I first met James O'Connell, afterwards Sir James, father of Sir Maurice the present baronet, and brother of the famous Dan O'Connell; a most agreeable man, full of interesting information and memories. Many a story he told me of his famous brother Dan; amongst them the following, which shows how unscrupulous O'Connell could be when he thought occasion required it. He had brought his brother either to the Bar of the House or behind the woolsack—I forget which—to hear a debate on Irish affairs in the House of Lords. A discussion arose on some petition which had been presented to the peers, in the course of which a Tory peer had said, "What are we to think, my lords, of such a petition as this, the first signature to which is that of Hamilton Rowan, an attainted traitor?"

Lord Brougham, seeing O'Connell, came down to him and said, "What am I to say to this?"

"You may say," said Dan, "that Mr. Hamilton Rowan never was an attainted traitor. It is true that in '98 he left Ireland for a little time; but on his return no charge was brought against him. He now holds a high position, is a magistrate of his county, and has twice served the office of high sheriff."

James was astounded, and as Brougham retired, caught his brother by the arm, saying, "Ah, Dan, Dan, I do not think he is a magistrate, or ever was high sheriff."

"Hold your tongue, you bosthoon!" said Dan. "What does it matter whether he was or not? If he wasn't, it will take three days to contradict it, and the whole business will be forgotten before that." There were no railways or telegraphs in those days.

Sir James also told me of a Mr. Tomkins Brew, a well-known and very popular magistrate in the county of Clare, who, when giving evidence before a committee of the House of Lords on crime in Ireland, was asked whether he knew much about the Roman Catholic priesthood. He replied, "I do not think, my lords, there is a man in Ireland that knows more about them than I do."

"I think I know a great deal about them, Mr. Brew," said Lord Roden.

"Ah! my lord," said Brew, "did you ever sleep between a parish priest and his coadjutor?"

Another of his stories was of a very conceited upstart young fellow, who, just after he had got a commission in the Cork Militia, was strutting about as proud as a peacock in his new uniform. He met a simple country lad, known as " Tom the fool." " I hardly think you know me, Tom," said he. " Bedad, I do know you," said Tom. " I'd know your skin on a bush; but I hardly think you know yourself, Masther Bob."

The same youth had, one morning, ordered his men to fall in for parade ; one fellow lagged behind, and was very slowly coming up when all the others were in position. " What are you dawdling there for, Sullivan?" said he; " fall in at once." " Begorra," answered Sullivan, " Masther Bob, you're in such a hurry you'd think the French was coming."

He told me also of the characteristic way in which an officer of the Ayrshire Fencibles, at one time quartered in the south, gave the order, " Right about face " to some recruits, whose left legs were marked with chalk, as was the custom then, to distinguish them from the right. He gave the word thus, " Ayrshire Fencibles, your back to the north, your face to the south, chalked leg foremost— MARCH!"

Sir James O'Connell was, what was rare in Ireland then, but far from uncommon now, a Conservative Roman Catholic. The last time I had the pleasure of meeting him was as we travelled together on the " Rakes of Mallow," a coach which plied daily between Cork and Mallow; he was going, he said, to consult his solicitor, as to whether he could bring an action against a priest who had, on the previous Sunday, denounced him in chapel about some land business; the chapel was on an outlying property of his, so he sent for one of his herds, who lived there, and asked, " Were you at Mass last Sunday ? "

Herd. " I was, yer honour."

Sir J. " Did Father S—— say anything about me ? "

Herd. " Well, he did mention your honour."

Sir J. " What did he say ? "

Herd. " Well now, your honour, I'm afeared you might be offinded if I tould you."

Sir J. " Not a bit. You must tell me at once, as exactly as you can, what he said."

Herd. " Well now, he told us all to go down on our knees, and pray to God to change the heart of that cruel, tyrannical old robber, James O'Connell."

Sir J. " What did you do ? "

Herd. " Why then, indeed, I went down on my knees and prayed strong for your honour."

On this same " Rakes of Mallow " coach I sometimes travelled with John Dillon Croker, of Quarterstown, a clever and useful county gentleman, but, without exception, the greatest talker I ever met; it was impossible " to get a word in edgeways." So great was his volubility that his own children could not sometimes help laughing at him, and the country people wondered "how he got wind for it all." One very wet morning he travelled inside the coach, while his son Harry and I, well wrapped up, were outside. When we stopped at Ballinamona to change horses, to our surprise out of the coach he came, and got up outside with us. "Why on earth, father," said Harry, "do you come out in this downpour?" "Indeed," said he, "there was an old lady in the coach who talked so much that I could stand it no longer." "Oh, father," said his son, "are you beaten at last?"

On another journey he said that a lady who was in the coach with him was the most agreeable fellow-passenger he had ever travelled with. The lady was deaf and dumb; he had not perceived it.

CHAPTER XII.

A proselytizing clergyman—Some examples of religious intolerance—An inverse repentance—The true faith—The railway mania—Famine of 1846—Mrs. Norton solves a difficulty—The old Beefsteak Club—A pleasant dinner-party.

In the year 1844 the rector of a parish near us was, on his death, succeeded by the Rev. Mr. A——, who shortly afterwards went in for proselytizing—a system which, as far as my experience goes, has never done the slightest good in Ireland, but often a great deal of harm by stirring up religious animosities, which have done endless mischief to our country, and which it ought to be the aim of every Irishman to allay. Since my early days I have seen a vast improvement in everything but intolerance in religion; that, I grieve to say, is as strong as ever. It is sad to-day to see our people still, as Lady Morgan says they were in her days—

" . . . a glorious nation,
A splendid peasantry on fruitful sod,
Fighting like divils for conciliation,
And hating one another for the love of God."

Mr. A——, with other proselytizing clergymen, of whom happily there were not many, did succeed in getting a few converts, such as they were; but in most cases, when they found that they did not obtain the temporal advantages which they supposed would follow their conversion, they soon returned to their former faith.

Many stories—how true I do not know—were told of Mr. A—— and his wonderful would-be converts. Here are two.

An old widow, Bryan, called on him, and on being shown into his library and asked by him what her business was, she said, "Well now, your raverence, it's what—I'd like to turn Protestant."

Mr. A. "Why do you wish to change your religion?"

Widow B. "Well now, I'm told 'your raverence gives a blanket and a leg of mutton to any one that turns.'"

Mr. A. "Do you mean to say that you would sell your soul for a blanket?"

Widow B. "No, your raverence, not without the leg of mutton."

Another day a countryman called on him and said, "I'm come to give myself up to your raverence because I'm unasy in my mind about my religion."

Mr. A. "What particular points are you uneasy about?"

Countryman. "Well now, your raverence, it's no

particular points that is throublin' me; it's a sort of giniral unaysiness."

On further questioning him it came out that what he really wanted was money or employment.

Mr. A. "I'll promise you nothing whatever. Do you think I'm like Mahomet, to take converts on any terms?"

Countryman. "And won't I get anything for turning?"

Mr. A. "Nothing. Go away; I'm ashamed of you."

Countryman. "Well, God bless your raverence anyway; and maybe your raverence would tell me where that Mr. Mahomet stops."

One of his converts, James Ryan, known as Jim Lar, I knew well. After trying Protestantism for a fortnight he had reverted to his ancient faith. "Jim Lar," I said to him, "you seem to be very unstable in your religious views. I hear you were a Protestant a fortnight ago, and that you are now again a Roman Catholic." "Well now, your honour," said he, "sure you wouldn't like me to be damning my soul and getting nothing for it."

I shall attempt to give a few odd examples of the height to which religious party feeling runs amongst the lower classes. Not very long ago an old Orangeman in the county of Down was asked, "Are the times as good now, Tom, as when you were a boy?" "Faith, they are not," answered Tom; "they'd take you up now and try you for shooting a Papist."

A farmer in the same county was summoned before a bench of magistrates for not having his name printed on the shaft of his cart; he said he didn't know it was the law, he was a loyal man, and wouldn't break the law on any account. They read him the section of the Act, which requires the name and address of the owner to be printed on the shaft " in Roman letters one inch long." " Roman letters !" said he. " Roman letters ! To hell with the pope ! "

A Roman Catholic clergyman told me of a woman in Cork who was complaining to her priest of the misconduct of her son; that he was always fighting, gambling, and drinking, and often beat her when he was drunk. " Ah," said the priest, "is he a Catholic at all?" " Begorra, your raverence," said she, " it's what he's too good a Catholic. If that boy had his will, he'd stick every Protestant from here to Tralee."

A Protestant clergyman, who had a living in the north of Ireland, on visiting one of his parishioners who was very ill, in fact on his death-bed, was told by the man that he was quite happy, and quite willing to die, but that there was one little thing annoying him for many years. The clergyman advised him not to worry himself about it, whatever it was; he was sure, if it was wrong, he had repented of it. " It's not troubling me, your raverence, in that way," said he; " it's only annoying me a wee bit. I'll tell your raverence what it is. In the big fight we had with the Papists thirty years ago, I had a priest covered with my gun, and something came over me that I didn't pull the trigger; and that's what's annoying me ever since."

In a well-known parish, in the province of Leinster, a handsome new church was built some thirty years ago. In the stained-glass window at the east end were the twelve apostles. Some of the Orangemen and extreme Low Churchmen in the parish, being scandalized at these (as they called them) "emblems of popery," smashed the windows. Many years after, an old parishioner, on his death-bed, said to the rector, who was visiting him, "Well, now, your raverence, hadn't we the real fun the day we broke the windows in the church?" "That was before my time," said the rector. "So it was, so it was," said the old man; "and more is the pity." Then he began to laugh, and added, "I stuck my stick right through St. Peter's eye."

The Rev. Doctor McGettigan, the late worthy Roman Catholic Bishop of Raphoe, often told of an incident which occurred when he was parish priest, I think, of Killybegs. "I was suddenly called," he said, "from my home to see an unfortunate sailor who had been cast ashore from a wreck, and was lying speechless on the ground, but not quite dead. The people standing by said, 'The life's in him still, your raverence; he stirred a little.' So I stooped down and said to him, 'My poor man, you're nearly gone; but just try to say one little word, or make one little sign to show that you are dying in the true faith.' So he opened one of his eyes just a wee bit, and he said, ' To hell with the pope ! ' and he died."

Another story of the bishop's, of quite a different kind, was this. He had slept one night at a farmhouse in a remote part of his diocese, and was awakened very early in the morning by some one calling out several times, " Who are you ?" To which he answered, "I am the most Reverend Doctor McGettigan, Bishop of Raphoe, the oldest bishop in Ireland ; indeed, I believe I may say the oldest bishop in Her Majesty's dominions." To which the same voice replied, " How is your mother ? " " My poor dear mother, God rest her soul ! " said the bishop, " died twenty years ago last Candlemas." The voice repeated twice in rapid succession, " How is your mother ? " He sat up in bed to see who the inquirer was, and beheld a grey parrot in a large cage by the window.

In the old days of the Orange Corporation in Dublin, the pedestal of the equestrian statue of William III. in College Green, was painted orange and blue. On the anniversary of the battle of the Boyne the statue was decked with orange lilies and orange ribbons, and on the pedestal, below the uplifted foot of the horse, was placed a bow of green ribbon. " Ah," said a man passing by, " see what respect the baste shows to the green ! See how he keeps his foot up in that unasy posture, for fear he might thrample on it ! "

Some pikes which had been found concealed were exhibited at a Conservative meeting in Dublin. Some one cried out, "A groan for the Pikes." A voice from the crowd replied, " A bloody end to them! "

Anything suggests politics. My father told me that at a theatre in Dublin, shortly after the Union, when a well-known actress was singing a favourite song, the refrain of which was " My heart goes pit-a-pat, pit-a-pat," a man from the gallery cried, " A groan for Pitt, and a cheer for Pat! "

In the year 1845 came the railway mania. Prospectuses in hundreds appeared, holding out the most enticing inducements to the public to take shares. One line was to develop the resources of Ballyhooly, a miserable village in the county of Cork; another to promote and encourage the cockle trade at Sandymount, where there is a strand on which, at low water, may be seen a dozen old women gathering cockles. All over the country, engineers and surveyors were levelling and surveying. One of these, an assistant of Sir John McNeill, was so engaged near Thurles, when a farmer, on whose land he was working, said to him, " May I make so bould, sir, as to ax what brings you here, and what you are doing?" "I'm laying out a railway," said he. "Begorra," said the farmer, " you are the fifth of them that has been here this week, and it's what it's my belief there isn't an idle blackguard in Dublin that has nothing to do that isn't sent down here to lay out railroads."

One of the surveyors was taking levels in a village, where the road was so steep that the levelling staff had to be held within a few yards of him. As he looked at the staff, which was held by one McEvoy, through the telescope of his level, he heard a woman at her cottage door calling to her husband, " Ah, then, Jim, come here and look at this. You never seen the like before. Here's a gintleman making a map of Mickey McEvoy."

Shortly before the years of famine, which began in 1846, our home at Abington was broken up by the death of my father. He died in 1845. Great as was his loss to us, I have often since felt glad that he was spared the grief and pain of those terrible years, when he would have had famine and fever on every side, and would have seen the poor people, to whom he had endeared himself by a thousand acts of kindness, and who were very dear to him, dying by hundreds around him, and enduring sufferings which, had he spent his all, as he would have gladly done, he would have been powerless to relieve.

During those years, though my residence was in Dublin, I travelled a great deal through the country, and witnessed many a heart-rending scene, never to be forgotten; but, as they would pain the feelings of my readers, I shall only relate the incidents of two consecutive days. As I, with my assistant engineer, was walking along the railway works which had just been commenced near Mallow, and which during the remainder of the famine gave much employment and relief, we passed near the old churchyard at Burnfort. Several dogs were fighting and howling there; my assistant ran down to see what they were about. He found them fighting over the bodies of some poor creatures who had died of famine, and had that morning been buried—if buried it can be called—without coffins, and so close to the surface, that they were barely covered with earth. We had coffins made for them, and had them buried at a proper depth. Next day, as I rode again from Cork to Mallow, I went into the Half-way House for a few minutes; a poor woman, barefooted and miserably clad, with three children, came in. So stricken with famine was she, that she could scarcely speak. I ordered coffee and bread for them. No sooner had she taken a little than she fainted. At first we thought she was dead, but after a little time we brought her round. The same night I had to start for London; and next evening saw a carpet spread across the footway to the carriage way, lest the damp should chill the feet or soil the shoes of some fashionable lady. The contrast was a painful one. Are there no such contrasts to-day within the great city itself?

It was on one of my visits to London later on— in the year 1861, I think—that I met my old friend, Mr. Fred. Ponsonby (now Lord Bessborough), in the lobby of the House of Commons. He asked me, if I had no other engagement, to dine with him at the Beefsteak Club on the following Saturday. "We dine," he said, "at the primitive hour of six; but you will get away at ten." I accepted his invitation with pleasure, and thought no more about it till the Saturday forenoon, when I turned to the directory to find the address of the club; but there was no mention of it there. I then made inquiries of some friends; some of them had never heard of it; others had, but did not know where it was. I was in a strait what to do. I did not know where Ponsonby was staying, so could not ask him. In my difficulty I bethought me of Mrs. Norton. "She will know, or will find out for me," I thought. So off to her house in Chesterfield Street I went. Fortunately I found her at home. I asked her if she knew anything about the club.

"I ought to know about it," she said, "for my father and my grandfather" (R. B. Sheridan) "were members of it. One of their rules is that they must meet under the roof of a theatre. They were burnt out of old Drury Lane, and out of other theatres, and where they now meet I do not know; but Cole will tell us." So she rang for Cole, her maid. When she appeared, Mrs. Norton said, "Cole, where does the Beefsteak Club dine at present?"

"At the Lyceum, ma'am," replied Cole. "You go in by a green door at the back of the theatre."

"That will do, Cole."

As soon as she had left the room I said, "In the

name of all that's wonderful, how does Cole know all this? Is she a witch?"

"Cole has changed her name since you saw her last," she said. "She is now Mrs. Smithson, though I still call her Cole. Her husband is a waiter, who attends dinner-parties, and I thought he might have told her something about this club."

At six o'clock I was at the green door, and on entering found my host and other members of the club, and two guests.

As the original club ceased to exist some five and twenty years ago, some account of my recollection of it may not be uninteresting to my readers. It consisted, I think, of twenty or four and twenty members, and my friend told me that latterly they seldom dined more than twelve or fourteen. The day I was there we were twelve, three of whom were guests—the late Lord Strathmore, who was, I think, made a member of the club that evening; Fechter, the famous actor; and myself. In the middle of the ceiling, over the dinner-table, was the original gridiron, which had been rescued from the ruins of the theatres out of which the club had been burnt. In large gold letters round the gridiron were the words, "BEEF AND LIBERTY." The same words were woven in the centre of the tablecloth, and engraved on all the plates and dishes, and they appeared again in gold on the wall at the end of the room, through a sort of portcullis in which you saw the beefsteaks being cooked. Over this portcullis were the words, "IF IT WERE DONE, WHEN 'TIS DONE, THEN 'TWERE WELL IT WERE DONE QUICKLY." With the exception of a welch-rarebit as second course, the dinner consisted of beefsteaks, and beefsteaks only. These came in in quick succession, two by two, one well done, the other rather under-done, so as to suit all palates. The drink was porter and port wine, which went round in flagons. The conversation was general, and full of fun.

After dinner the chairman brewed a huge bowl of punch—whether of brandy or of whisky, I forget; the vice-chairman a smaller one of rum. From the bowls jugs were filled, one of which was placed before each of those at table. There were about the room many old theatrical properties of various sorts; amongst them dresses which had been worn by actors famous in days of yore.

The chairman wore a cloak and hat which Garrick had worn in *Hamlet*. There were only two or three toasts proposed, one of which was the health of the guests. After this had been drunk with enthusiasm, the chairman said, "It is the custom here that the guests shall rise and return thanks simultaneously." We three rose and declared simultaneously, but each in his own words, how deeply we felt the kind manner in which our health had been drunk. The chairman then rose again and said, "I now propose that the excellent speeches, which have just been delivered by our eloquent guests, be printed and circulated at the expense of the club. As many as are of that opinion will say, 'Aye.'" There was a chorus of "Ayes." "As many as are of the contrary opinion will say, 'No.'" Not a single "No," or dissentient voice. Whereupon the chairman solemnly said, "The 'Noes' have it." After that, till ten o'clock, "the night drave on wi' sangs and clatter," when we separated, after as pleasant an evening as I ever spent.

CHAPTER XIII.

Smith O'Brien's rebellion—Louis Philippe's interview with the Queen, as seen by the boy Jones—Plain fare and pleasant—Married by mistake—A time for everything—A pagan altar-piece—Drawing the long-bow—Proof against cross-examination — Fooling the English — Larceny or trespass?

IN 1848 I went to live at Rathpeacon House, near Cork, as I was then engaged in carrying out the completion of the Great Southern and Western Railway to that city.

At the time of my arrival, the French Revolution had just broken out, and all through the south, especially in "Rebel Cork," there was the wildest excitement. A rebellion under Smith O'Brien and the other Young Ireland leaders was daily expected. A revolution in England, too, was hoped for; but this hope was extinguished by the suppression of the great Chartist meeting in London, and all chance of a successful rebellion in Ireland ended with the arrest of Smith O'Brien and the dispersion of his followers, after the abortive rising at Slievenaman. It was here that, on being ordered to attack a police barrack garrisoned by half a dozen constables, his gallant troops replied, "Is it what your honour wants us, to go up there to be shot?" and thereupon fled, leaving their general alone.

In Cork many Young Irelanders were arrested, amongst them a friend of mine, Michael Joseph Barry, a clever young barrister, who had written some stirring songs and pleasant Irish stories, and whom I visited several times when he was in prison.

It will be remembered that about that time a boy named Jones had been found two or three times concealed in Buckingham Palace, not, as it came out, with any felonious intentions, but simply from curiosity. It will also be remembered that when Louis Philippe fled from France, nothing was heard of him for some days; and as all the world wondered what had become of him, Barry wrote the following squib, supposed to be from the boy Jones, which appeared in the *Southern Reporter*, then, as now, an influential Liberal newspaper in Cork:—

"THE FRENCH REVOLUTION.

"To the Editor of the *Southern Reporter*.

"Mr. EDITOR,

"My mother being a Blackpool woman, I wish to give you the first news of what happened between Louis Philippe and her Grayshus Majesty. I was behind a curtain listenin' to the dialogue on Friday evening.

'My dear Vic, ses he,
I'm mighty sick, ses he,
For I've cut my stick, ses he,
Tarnation quick, ses he,

From the divil's breeze, ses he,
At the Tooleyrees, ses he;
For the blackguards made, ses he,
A barricade, ses he.
They're up to the trade, ses he,
And I was afraid, ses he,
And greatly in dread, ses he,
I'd lose my head, ses he;
And if I lost that, ses he,
I'd have no place for my hat, ses he.

'Stop a while, ses she;
Take off your tile, ses she.
You're come a peg down, ses she,
By the loss of your crown, ses she.

'Mille pardon, ses he,
For keepin' it on, ses he;
But my head isn't right, ses he,
Since I took to flight, ses he;
For the way was long, ses he,
And I'm not over sthrong, ses he.

'Indeed, my ould buck, ses she,
You look mighty shuck, ses she.

'You may say I am, ses he;
I'm not worth a damn, ses he,
Till I get a dhram, ses he,
And a cut of mate, ses he;
For I'm dead bate, ses he.
I'm as cowld as ice, ses he.

'Never say it twice, ses she;
I'll get you a slice, ses she,
Of something nice, ses she;
And we'll make up a bed, ses she,
In the room overhead, ses she.

'I like a mathrass, ses he,
　Or a pallyass, ses he;
　But in my present pass, ses he,
　Anything of the kind, ses he,
　I shouldn't much mind, ses he.'

"Here a grand waither dhressed all in goold brought in the ateables. Her Majesty helped Looey to some cowld ham, which he tucked in as if he hadn't tasted a bit since he left the Tooleyrees. By degrees he lost his appetite and found his tongue, but he didn't like talking while the waither was there, so he touched her Majesty, and ses he in an undertone—

'Bid that flunkey go, ses he,
　And I'll let you know, ses he,
　About my overthrow, ses he.'

"So the Queen made a sign with her hand, and the flunkey tuck himself off with a very bad grace, as if he'd have liked to be listening. When the door was shut Looey went on—

'"Twas that Guizot, ses he—
　That chap you knew, ses he,
　When we were at Eu, ses he,
　At our interview, ses he.

'Is that thrue? ses she.
　I thought he and you, ses she,
　Were always as thick, ses she,
　As——

'Don't say pickpockets, Vic, ses he.
　Indeed, we wor friends, ses he,
　And had the same ends, ses he,
　Always in view, ses he;
　But we little knew, ses he,
　That a Paris mob, ses he,
　Would spoil our job, ses he.
　They're the divil's lads, ses he—
　What you call Rads, ses he;
　But your Rads sing small, ses he,

Before powdher and ball, ses he,
While mine don't care a jot, ses he,
For round or grape shot, ses he.
Well, those chaps of mine, ses he,
They wanted to dine, ses he,
And to raise up a storm, ses he,
About getting reform, ses he;
Which isn't the thing, ses he,
For a citizen king, ses he,
Or a well-ordhered state, ses he,
To tolerate, ses he.
So says I to Guizot, ses he,
We must sthrike a blow, ses he.
Ses Guizot, You're right, ses he,
For they'll never fight, ses he;
They're sure to be kilt, ses he,
By them forts you built, ses he;
And the throops is thrue, ses he,
And they'll stand to you, ses he.
Then ses I to Guizot, ses he,
Proclaim the Banquo, ses he,
And let them chaps know, ses he,
That Reform's no go, ses he.
But bad luck to our haste, ses he,
For stoppin' the faste, ses he,
For the people riz, ses he.
And that's how it is, ses he,
That you find me here, ses he,
At this time of year, ses he,
Hard up for a bed, ses he,
To rest my head, ses he.

'Did you save your tin? ses she.

'Did I? (with a grin), ses he.
Faix, it's I that did, ses he,
For I had it hid, ses he,
Lest a storm should burst, ses he,
To be fit for the worst, ses he.

"Here Looey stopped, and little Lord Johnny, who had been peepin' in at the door, walked into the room, just as the Queen, who had caught sight of him, put up her finger for him to come in. Looey rose up to meet him.

> 'Are you there, ses he,
> My little Premier? ses he.
> Gad! you're lookin' ill, ses he.
> Troth, I am, King Phil, ses he.
> Would you cash a bill, ses he,
> For a couple of mille? ses he.
> I've no tin in the till, ses he.
> Good night, ses Phil, ses he.
> I've a cowld in my head, ses he,
> And I'll go to bed, ses he.'

"And he walked out of the room in a great hurry, leaving Lord Johnny in a great foosther, and indeed her Majesty didn't look over well pleased; but there the matter ended.

"P.S.—You'll hear that Looey wasn't in London at all, but you may thrust to the thruth of the above.

"Yours to command,
"THE BOY JONES."

It was some time after this a western member of Parliament, who thought he knew French well, went to Paris, with a deputation of Irishmen to present an address to Louis Napoleon. The member of Parliament addressed Napoleon in French, but had not gone far when Napoleon said he must ask him to be so good as to speak English, which he understood, as he did not understand Irish.

About a mile from my house at Rathpeacon lived Father Horgan, the good old parish priest of Blarney, a fine sample of a Roman Catholic priest of former days, and as worthy a man as ever lived. He was well known as an Irish scholar and antiquarian, and such was his interest in and love for the old round towers of Ireland that he determined to build a fac-simile of one in his chapel-yard as a mausoleum for himself. It is not, however, so like its prototype as he meant it to be. The difference arose in this way. A large subscription had been made in the parish for its erection, and Father Horgan rashly began to build before he had sufficiently considered whether he had enough to finish. When the tower had risen to one-half its height the funds began to fail, and as he either could not or would not raise more money in the parish, he had to cut his coat according to his cloth, and was forced to diminish its diameter. Its appearance as it stands is not unlike that of a gigantic champagne bottle.

Father Horgan was the soul of hospitality, and gave many a dinner-party, where all sorts and conditions of men were wont to meet; at the upper end of his table were clergy and gentry of the neighbourhood, peasant farmers at the lower. The eatables were alike for all—alternate dishes of chicken and bacon all down the table. With the drinkables it was different; there was wine at the upper end, whisky (which they preferred) for the farmers at the lower. He said to me, "You see, my dear friend, I don't know how to order a big dinner with all sorts of dishes; and if I did, old Bridget could not cook it. So I just have a pair of chickens and then a dish of bacon and greens, then another pair of chickens and another dish of bacon and greens, and so on all the way down. Every one likes chickens and bacon, and when a man sees these before him he looks for nothing else. I am saved a world of trouble, and every one seems happy and contented." And so they were, and right pleasant those homely dinners were—quite as pleasant as those given by a Mr. A——, a wealthy solicitor in Dublin, famous for his cook and for the excellence and abundance of his wine, especially his claret.

A few of the most agreeable men in Dublin met at one of these parties and spent a thoroughly enjoyable evening. A few days afterwards Chief Justice Doherty, who had been one of the guests, met Mr. A——, and said to him, " What a pleasant party we had with you last Tuesday ! " " Do you call that a pleasant party ? " said A——. " *I* don't." " Why not ? " said Doherty. " Too much talk, too much talk; you couldn't enjoy your wine; you drank little more than a bottle each. On Wednesday I had nine men to dinner, and they drank three bottles a man ; and you'd have heard a pin drop the whole time. That's what *I* call a pleasant party."

Amongst my friends in Cork was another priest, Father O'Sullivan, generally known as " Father Rufus " from his red hair. He gave me the following account of a wedding at which he was called upon to officiate in a hurry. Just as he had put on his hat and coat and was leaving his house to drive to Passage, where he was engaged to dine, a young couple met him at his door and said they had come to be married; they showed him their papers of authority for him to marry them, which were all right. He told them to come early next morning, as he was in too great a hurry then; but they said they were in a greater hurry, as they were going to America, and had to start for Liverpool by the Cork steamer that evening. So he brought them into his sitting-room, told them to kneel down, and commenced to read the service. When he had gone on for a while the young man said, "I don't know, your raverence, whether it makes any difference, but I'm only a witness in the case. The boy himself will be here directly." I am greatly afraid, from what Father Rufus told me, the ceremony had gone so far that the witness, before he had interrupted, was married to the girl; but if this was so it never was divulged. The right boy very soon arrived, the ceremony was performed *de novo*, and the happy bride, with her husband (number two), was in time for the Liverpool boat. Not so lucky was his reverence, who was much put out by losing his good dinner at Passage. Priests are, after all, but men, and dislike as much as others being disturbed just at or immediately before or after meal-times.

Father H——, the pleasantest of all priests, past or present, gave me an instance of this kind, when his temper was sorely tried. Amongst his parishioners, was Tom Burns, a drunken fellow, who, when in his cups, was violent, and often beat his wife. One cold and stormy winter's evening, Father H——, having had his dinner, had settled himself snugly by his bright fireside, and was just brewing his tumbler of whisky punch, when his servant rushed into his room, crying out, " Your raverence is wanted out instantly. Tom Burns is killing his wife, and if you're not there at once she will be dead." Down he ran to the cottage, and on his arrival found that they had succeeded in quieting Tom, who was lying in a state of drunken exhaustion on his bed. Father H—— was in no frame of mind to speak gently to him; his language, I fear, was not quite clerical, " blackguard," " drunken ruffian" being about his mildest expressions. Tom turned his face to the wall, and in a meek and humble voice said, " Go away, your raverence, go away. I'm not in a fit state to listen to your holy voice."

To return to Father Rufus. One of his oldest friends was Father Prout, the eccentric parish priest of Ardnagehy, in the county of Cork; it was from him that Father Frank Mahony took his well-known *nom de plume*, under which he wrote so charmingly. When Father Rufus was in Rome studying for the Church, old Prout came there to purchase an altar-piece for his chapel—a subscription had been raised for the purpose—and called on him to ask his assistance and advice. He went with him to many dealers and artists whom he knew; but, after a long day's search, nothing was found to satisfy his friend. A few days afterwards Prout called again to say he had just found exactly what he wanted; but, before buying it, he would like Father Rufus to see it, and give his opinion. When he saw it he exclaimed, "Why, man, that is a Diana!" "I don't care what it is," said Prout; "it's lovely, and I'll have it; those chaps of mine at Ardnagehy will never know the difference."

In giving answers the Irish peasantry, as a rule, have no great regard for truth, but like to give the answer which they think will be most agreeable to the questioner. A poor Italian organ-grinder, weary after the long walk, asked a peasant whom he met near Carrigtuohil how far he was from Cork. "Just four short miles," was the answer. "What do you mean," said Father Rufus, who happened to pass at the time, "by deceiving the poor fellow? You know well enough it's eight long miles." "Sure, your raverence," said the other, "I seen the poor boy was tired, and I wanted to keep his courage up. If he heard your raverence—but I'm plazed to think he didn't—he'd be down-hearted entirely."

A story which is well known in Kerry was told me long ago by a Mr. R——, of Tralee. He was shooting with an English friend, a Mr. B——. They had very little sport; so Mr. B—— said, "I'll ask this countryman whether there are any birds about here." "No use to ask him," said Mr. R——; "he'll only tell you lies." "I'll ask him, at all events," said Mr. B——. "My good man, are there any birds about here?" "Lots of birds, your honour," said he. "Tell me what sort of birds?" "Well now, your honour, there's grouses, and woodcocks, and snipes, and ducks, and pillibines, and all sorts of birds." "Ask him," whispered R——, "whether there are any thermometers." "Tell me," said B——, "do you ever see any thermometers here?" "Well now, your honour, if there was a night's frost, the place would be alive with them."

Many years afterwards, as I drove with my wife from Killarney to Kenmare, I told her this story. She said she could hardly believe it. I said, "I'll try with this boy, and you'll see he'll say much the same." So I said to the bare-legged boy who was running along beside the carriage—

"What is the name of the little river near us?"

Boy. "'Tis the Finnhry, your honour."

"Are there many fish in it?"

Boy. "There is, your honour."

"What sort of fish?"

Boy. "There do be throuts and eels, your honour."

"Any salmon?"

Boy. "There do be an odd one."

"Any white trout?"

Boy. "There do be a good lot of them."

"Any thermometers?"

Boy. "Them does be there, too, your honour; but they comes up lather in the season than the white throuts."

At Carrigtuohil, which I mentioned just now, I got a curious answer. It often is hard to get from a peasant the meaning of the Irish name of a place. This probably arises from the name having been a good deal changed from what it originally had been. For instance, "Tipperary" was originally Tubber Ara (the Well of Ara); "Raduane" was Rathduffown (the Fort of the Black River). I asked a country fellow, "What is the English of Carrigtuohil?" "I never heard any English or Irish name upon it, only Carrigtuohil alone," said he. "I know," said I, "it has no other name, but I want to know the meaning of the name." "Well now, your honour," he answered, "I never heard any meaning for it only Carrigtuohil alone." "I know 'Carrig' means a rock," I said; "but what does 'tuohil' mean?" "Well now, your honour, it's what I can't tell you why it's called Carrigtuohil, unless it's because Mr. Coppinger lives below there in Barry's Court."

Amongst the leading counsel engaged for and against the Great Southern Railway Company, who were purchasing land for their line in the county of Tipperary, were Fitzgibbon and Rolleston. They, with two or three others, were out for a walk, one fine Sunday afternoon, and sat down to rest on a sunny bank in a field near Templemore.

Rolleston pointed out the spot in an adjoining field where a Mr. E—— had been murdered some time before. Two men had been tried for the murder, but were not convicted, though it was well known through the country that they were the murderers. Rolleston had been counsel for the prosecution.

"Ah," said Fitzgibbon, "if I had been in that case I'd have got a conviction."

"Why do you think so?" said Rolleston.

"Because," said Fitzgibbon, "I would have broken down the witnesses for the defence on cross-examination. I never saw a lying witness that I could not break down."

It was quite true that Fitzgibbon was a very powerful cross-examiner; but it was supposed that he somewhat overrated his powers.

"Well," said Rolleston, "try your hand on that boy standing over there; you may be sure he knows all about the murder; and I'll bet you a pound you won't get any satisfactory information about it from him."

"Done," said Fitzgibbon. "Come here, my boy. Do you live near here?"

Boy. "I do, your honour; I live in that house below there."

Fitzgibbon. "Do you know Mr. E——?"

Boy. "I do not, sir."

Fitzgibbon. "I heard he lived near this."

Boy. "So he did, your honour, in that big white house."

Fitzgibbon. "Then how is it you don't know him?"

Boy. "Because he is dead, sir."

Fitzgibbon. "I'm sorry to hear that, but are you sure he is dead?"

Boy. "Didn't I see him dead?"

Fitzgibbon. "Where?"

Boy. "In that field below, your honour."

Fitzgibbon. "Did you perceive anything particular about him?"

Boy. "I did."

Fitzgibbon. "What was it?"

Boy. "He was lying in a lough of blood, sir."

Fitzgibbon. "Then perhaps he had been killed?"

Boy. "Begorra, he was killed, your honour."

Fitzgibbon. "Now, like a good boy, tell me did you ever hear how, or by whom, he was killed?"

Boy. "I did, your honour."

Hereupon Fitzgibbon looked triumphantly at Rolleston; and, confident that he would win his bet, said to the boy—

"Now, tell me exactly what you heard?"

"Well, your honour, I heard it was what he fell asleep in the field, and a weazel sucked him."

Upon this there was such a laugh at Fitzgibbon, that he gave up his examination, and handed a pound to Rolleston.

I heard a very bullying counsel, Deane Freeman, completely put out in his cross-examination by a very simple answer.

Freeman (*to Witness*). "So you had a pistol?"

Witness. "I had, sir."

Freeman. "Who did you intend to shoot with it?"

Witness. "I wasn't intending to shoot no one."

Freeman. "Then was it for nothing that you got it?"

Witness. "No, it wasn't."

Freeman. "Come, come, sir, on the virtue of your solemn oath, what did you get that pistol for?"

Witness. "On the virtue of my solemn oath, I got it for three and ninepence in Mr. Richardson's shop." (Much laughter in court.)

Freeman. "Oh, how very witty you are! You may go down."

At another time he said to a witness, "You're a nice fellow, ain't you?" Witness replied, "I am a nice fellow; and if I was not on my oath, I'd say the same of you."

I was told of another witness, a labouring man, whose answers on his direct examination were rather discursive. He was asked by the cross-examining counsel, "Now, my good man, isn't all this that you have been telling to my friend here only a hypothesis?"

Witness. "Well, if your honour says so, I suppose it was."

Counsel. "Come, sir, on your oath, do you know what a hypothesis is?"

Witness. "Well, now, I think I do."

Counsel. "Then tell me what it is?"

Witness. "Well, now, I think it's some part of the inside of a pig, but I'm not exactly shure what part it is."

Judge Burton, who was a very old and wizened little man, was trying a case, when another very old man, scarcely able to walk, came into court to give evidence. Instead of going to the witness-box, he went towards the passage leading to the bench. McDonagh, the counsel, called out to him, "Come back, sir. Where are you going? Do you think you are a judge?" "Indeed, sir," said the old man, looking up at Judge Burton—"indeed, sir, I believe I am fit for little else."

It is sometimes hard to say whether such answers are given in truthful simplicity or not; but certainly the peasants, particularly in the south, do like to take in a stranger. A nephew of mine was staying with me, some years ago, at my fishing quarters in Kerry. In the evening of the day he had arrived he told me that young Dan Neale, then my fishing boy, or gillie, had given him a wonderful account of an enormous eel, which ran ashore near Blackwater Pier. It was very nearly as thick as a horse, and it had a great mane on its neck; he and a dozen of the other men and boys had great work in killing it with spades and shovels.

"He was humbugging you," said I.

"No," said he. "It must be true; he told me every detail about it, and the names of some of the men who helped to kill it, and he was perfectly serious at the time."

Next morning, when Dan appeared, I called him up before my nephew, and said, "Dan Neale, did you ever see an enormous eel run ashore at Blackwater Pier?"

"I never did, your honour," said Dan.

"Then why did you tell me that long story about it?" said my nephew.

"To be making a fool of your honour," said Dan.

When I told this to my old friend, the late Mr. Valentine O'Connor, he gave me the following account of how a young English lady, who had never been in Ireland before, was made a fool of by a Kingstown car-driver. O'Connor, who lived near Blackrock, about two miles from Kingstown, was expecting the arrival from England of a governess for his daughters. He and Mrs. O'Connor had just sat down to breakfast when an outside car drove past the window to the hall door, the young governess sitting up on high in the driver's seat, while he sat on the side of the car. On inquiry, it came out that on leaving Kingstown the driver was sitting on one side (as they often do), and the young lady on the other. She pointed to the driving seat, and said to him, "Carman, what is that seat there for?" "Well, my lady," said he, "that sate up there is mostly for tourists. They gets a betther view of the country from it than they would from the side of the car. We mostly charges them a shilling extra for it, but you seem to be such a plasin' young lady that you may get up into it for sixpence." So she paid him sixpence and got up.

Amongst those who afforded amusement to their neighbours in Cork was an old lady, Miss McCall, generally known as "Betty McCall," who, with her niece, lived at a very pretty place near Glanmire. She was very tenacious of her rights, and was known to wander about with a large horse-pistol in her hand in quest of trespassers. She heard that some of her neighbours, amongst them being Mr. Abbott the Quaker, were in the habit of bathing, early in the morning, in the river that passed through her grounds. This annoyed and shocked her much, and finding that notices threatening prosecution were posted up in vain, she told her gardener she would not keep him unless by some means he put a stop to these dreadful practices. Having turned the matter over in his mind, he thought the most effectual way would be to conceal himself and watch for bathers and take away their clothes. One morning, as Betty and her niece Lizzie were sitting in their bow-window at their early breakfast, a tall and portly figure, devoid of clothing, passed the window and rang violently at the hall door, which was quickly opened by her maid, but still more quickly shut; whereupon Mr. Abbott, for it was he, put his mouth to the keyhole and called out, "Tell Betty McCall that Brother Abbott, having done nothing whereof to be ashamed, has come to ask for his clothes."

Betty took out a summons against Abbott for trespass, he against her for larceny of his clothes. Much amusement was expected in court, but neither case ever came on, as, through the interference of friends, a compromise was effected.

CHAPTER XIV.

Anthony Trollope: his night encounter—A race for life on an engine—Railway adventures—I become Commissioner of Public Works—Some Irish repartees and ready car-drivers —Rail against road—No cause for uneasiness.

IT was in Cork I first met Anthony Trollope, who was then an *employé* in the Post-office Department. He gave me the following account of his first visit to Ireland. He had been ordered to proceed at once to a remote village in the far west, to make inquiries respecting irregularities in the post-office there. After a weary journey, he arrived late in the afternoon at his destination, and had to put up at a small public-house, the only place of entertainment in the village. His bedroom was approached by a flight of steps, half stairs, half ladder, not far from perpendicular. The room was scantily furnished; it contained two beds close together, a table, a chair, and a basin-stand. Weary, after his long journey on the outside of a coach, he retired early, and tried to fasten his door, but found he could not, as it had neither lock nor bolt. When he went to bed it was some time before he slept, as he felt nervous and uncomfortable in this strange, wild place. At last he fell into an uneasy restless sort of sleep, and did not know how long he had been sleeping, when he suddenly woke up and heard a footstep stealthily approaching his bed. Frightened, and but half awake, he sprang from his bed, seized the intruder, and found himself grappling with a powerful man, clad, like himself, only in his shirt, whom he held so tightly by the throat that he could not speak. In their struggle they came to the open door, where his antagonist stumbled and fell down the stairs.

Aroused by the noise of the struggle and fall, the inmates of the house rushed into the room and struck a light. The moment they had done so Trollope heard his landlady cry out—

"Oh, boys, that murderin' villain upstairs has killed his raverence!"

"We'll soon settle the b—— sassenach," said the men, rushing to the steps; and but for the intervention of the half-strangled priest, who had now come to himself, Trollope would, no doubt, have been lynched.

When peace was established, apologies made and accepted, and an explanation given, he found that the man he had assaulted was the parish priest, who, having been kept out at a late call in this remote part of his parish, had come into the public-house to get a bed. Hearing that an English gentleman was occupying the other bed in the room, he went up as noiselessly as possible, undressed, put out his candle, and was creeping to bed as softly as he could, lest he should disturb the sleeping stranger. He was amazed when he was seized by the throat and flung down the stairs. Fortunately he was none the worse for his fall, and he and Trollope became fast friends. After some time, when they met again, they had a hearty laugh over their first acquaintance.

During my residence in Cork, and for many years afterwards, I constantly travelled on engines, and though I never met with any accident worth speaking of, I ran some risks, of which the following are a few examples.

One pitch-dark night I had rather an unpleasant ride from the Limerick junction to Charleville. The line of railway from Dublin to Cork was nearly finished; a single line of rails had just been roughly laid to Charleville, and two engines were employed in ballasting the line and in drawing waggon-loads of rails and sleepers. One of the engines, called the "William Dargan," after the contractor, was a large and powerful one; the other, much smaller, was named the "Lady MacNeill," after the wife of Sir John MacNeill, the engineer.

I was staying at Charleville, and had to attend a trial in the town of Tipperary. I told Robert Edwards, the contractor's engineer—a wild, reckless young fellow he then was—to have the little engine ready at the junction at eight in the evening, to take me back to Charleville. I was kept later in Tipperary than I had expected, and did not get to the junction till after half-past eight. We got up on the engine and started, Edwards driving at a great pace.

"Better not go so fast, Edwards," said I; "the road is very rough, and we'll be off as sure as fate."

"I know the road is rough," said he; "but it's better to run the chance of being killed that way, than to be surely killed the other way if we go slow."

"What other way?" I asked.

"Why," he said, "I told the 'William Dargan' to start from Charleville, with a rake of empty waggons, exactly at nine o'clock, if we weren't in before that, and if we don't run fast she'll be into us, and send us to glory."

"Better go back to the junction, and wait till she comes," I suggested.

"Never fear," he said. "It's only twenty miles; I'll do it in time."

So on we went, the engine jumping, and every minute swaying from side to side; two or three times I was certain we were off the line. I may say we were running for our lives, for when we arrived the big engine had actually whistled, and in half a minute would have started.

A few days later things did not turn out so favourably. Either through some misdirection or the misunderstanding of directions, the two engines did meet on the line. Edwards and an assistant of his, named Mulqueen, with the driver and fireman, were on the small engine—I was not, luckily for me, able to go with them that morning. Just as they came out of a cutting they saw the big engine coming towards them at full speed. "Make your soul, Mulqueen; we're done," said Edwards. The driver reversed the engine and put on the break, and just before the "William Dargan" was upon them they jumped off, and all escaped unhurt except Mulqueen, who had his arm broken. The weight of the large engine threw the little "Lady MacNeill" off the line and down an embankment, at the foot of which she lay, much shattered, on her side; the "William Dargan" held its own, and none of those on it were hurt.

One night, near Thurles, some one, either for mischief or for sport, dropped a huge stone from the parapet of a bridge on the engine. It struck the fireman, who fell insensible on the foot-plate. We thought at first that he was killed, but he soon revived; his head was badly cut and his collar-bone broken.

Another time, when the line from Waterford to Tramore was just finished, I was riding on the engine, when we saw a boy placing a very large stone, which he could scarcely carry, on the rail. He then stood beside the line watching for the result. We pulled up as quickly as possible, and were going comparatively slow when we reached the stone, which the iron guard in front of the wheel threw off the line. We stopped the engine, jumped off, and gave chase to the boy, whom we very soon captured. He was a small boy about ten years old. We led him back, weeping piteously, and took him up on the engine. He besought us not to kill him. We told him we would not kill him, but that we would bring him into Waterford, where he would be tried, and undoubtedly hanged next morning for trying to kill us. When we had gone about half a mile we stopped and let him off; and didn't the little chap run! He evidently feared lest we should change our minds again and deliver him up to the hangman.

The railway between Bagnalstown and Kilkenny, of which I was engineer, was a single line. One morning a regiment—I think a battalion of the Rifle Brigade—was to leave Kilkenny for Bagnalstown. Owing to some mistake as to his orders, the stationmaster started a heavy goods train from the latter town, and telegraphed to the station-master at Kilkenny, "Don't start the soldiers till the goods train which I have just started arrives." The reply he got was, "Your goose is cooked; the soldiers have started." Fortunately the trains came in sight of each other on a long, straight part of the line; but even so the drivers were barely able to pull up in time to prevent a collision. Had they met anywhere else, an accident would have been inevitable.

In 1853 I again took up my abode in Dublin. I was sorry to leave Cork, where I had spent five happy years amongst some of the kindest and most hospitable people in Ireland, and where I had had plenty of salmon and trout fishing in the Lee and other rivers, and, as I had leave to shoot on all the neighbouring properties, capital snipe shooting too.

The next ten years were the busiest of my life. During them I was engineer to many railways and other important works, and so continued, with the additional duties of engineer to the Irish Light Railway Board, till 1863, when I was offered the appointment of Commissioner of Public Works in Ireland, which I accepted, having been much pressed to do so by my friends in the Irish Government.

My work as an engineer involved much travelling by coach and car in country and in town, and many a pleasant driver I have met. One old fellow had driven me to my office on a bitterly cold winter's morning. I arrived in a snowstorm, and never did I see such a picture of cold as the poor old man; his whiskers and his beard stiff with frost and snow, and a miniature icicle depending from his nose. Having paid him his fare, I said to him (a little unfeelingly perhaps), "I hope the midges are not biting you this morning." "Bedad, they are, your honour," he answered; "an' it's what I think this hate will be for thunder."

On Knockacuppal Hill, a very steep one on the road from Mallow to Killarney, a small boy clad in only one garment—an old corduroy jacket—used to run after the coach as it went slowly up the hill, asking for pennies. I heard an English lady, who was on the box-seat beside the coachman, say to him, "Isn't it very sad to see that poor little fellow with nothing on him but that wretched little jacket?" "Ma'am," said the coachman, "that boy could have clothes enough if he choose." "And why hasn't he?" she said. "Well now, ma'am, that boy is so wonderful ticklesome that he never could stand to let a tailor take his measure for a pair of trousers."

The Rev. Dr. Marshall, a well-known convert to Rome, who was a very large man, about nineteen or twenty stone weight, had been attending a meeting at the Rotunda, in Dublin, and took a covered car to go to Drumcondra, where he was staying. Before he got into the car he asked the driver to tell him what the fare was.

Driver. "I'll l'ave that to you, your raverence."

Dr. Marshall. "But how much is it?"

Driver. "Whatever your raverence plazes."

Dr. Marshall. "That won't do. I shall not get into the car till you tell me the fare."

Driver. "Get in at once, your raverence, for if the horse turns and gets a sight of you, the divil a step he'll go at all."

The late Father O'Dwyer, parish priest of Enniskerry, gave a carman, who had driven him home on a wet day, a glass of whisky. He begged for another glass. Father O'Dwyer, who knew that the man was rather too fond of spirits, refused, and, still holding the decanter in his hand, said, "Every glass of that you drink is a nail in your coffin." "Why, then, your raverence," said the man, "as you have the hammer in your hand, you might as well drive another nail into it."

Another priest having given a glass of whisky to a carman who complained of not feeling well, said to him, "How do you feel now? Didn't that make another man of you?" "Bedad, it did, your raverence; and the other man would like a glass too."

An old lady getting into a cab in Grafton Street, in Dublin, was heard to say to the driver, "Help me to get in, my good man, for I'm very old." "Begorra, ma'am," said he, "no matter what age you are, you don't look it."

But of all the carmen I have met, George Cullen of Bray is my favourite. There is a kindliness and simplicity about him that is quite refreshing. Paul Cullen, I used to call him, after the Roman Catholic Archbishop of Dublin, Cardinal Paul Cullen. The carmen at Bray, too, often called him Paul, and, on my arrival from Dublin at the railway station, would call to him, "Paul, here's the masther waiting for you." One windy day his hat was blown off, and one of them said to him, "Begorra, Paul, you were very nearly losing your mitre." Some time after I had given up my profession, and become Commissioner of Public Works, I was driving home on his car, when we had the following conversation :—

Cullen. "Does your honour get your health as well now as when you would be making them railroads?"

I. "Yes, Paul; thank God, I am as well as ever I was."

Cullen. " Does your honour make as much money ?"

I. " No, Paul, I am sorry to say I do not."

Cullen. "But I suppose, your honour, the situation is more respectable like ? "

Another time he told me of a ghost that was occasionally seen at a well near Bray Commons.

" It was," he said, " the spirit of a poor man that was run over and his head cut off him by the Waxford Coach."

" Did you ever see it, Paul ? " said I.

" Well now, your honour, I got a sight of it the other night when I was afther laving you and the misthress at home from Judge Crampton's. It was standing near the well."

I. " What was it like ? "

Cullen. " Well, it was in the form of a man."

I. " Did you speak to it ? "

Cullen. " The Lord forbid that I'd spake to it."

I. " Did it not speak to you, Paul ? "

Cullen. " It didn't speak to me, your honour ; but it made a terrible buzz out of it, like as if a big bee would be flying a-past you ; and away I dhrove home as fast as I could pelt."

On a wet and warm summer's day, as he drove me home, I told him that if we were able to get above the clouds we should find it a lovely bright, cold day, and as we went higher it would grow colder and colder, until, if we got up high enough, we should be frozen to death. " I got a skitch of that the other day, your honour," said Paul. "There were two gentlemen, tourists I think they wor; I drove them all round by Delgany and the Glin of the Downs, and they were spaking about them things—balloons I think they call them—and one of them said he went up in one of them not long since, and first he kem into a hot climate, and then into a cowld climate, and above that again he got into a climate of flies, and overhead, above all, saving your honour's presence, he said he got up into a stinkin climate. That's the way I got a skitch of it."

When the railway between Dublin and Drogheda —one of the first in Ireland—was in course of construction, I constantly travelled between these places on the Drogheda coach, of which old Peter Pentlebury, an Englishman with an Irish wife, was the coachman. He would never bring himself to believe that the line would be finished, so for a time he was pleasant and chatty; but as he saw the works coming towards completion he grew morose, and would scarcely speak a word to any one connected with them.

The day the first engine ran from Drogheda to Dublin, as Sir John MacNeill and I were standing on the foot-plate of the engine, we saw the coachman's wife on the platform.

"Come along, Mrs. Pentlebury," said Sir John, "and we'll give you the fastest drive to Dublin you ever had."

"But how can I get down again?" said she.

"We'll bring you in in plenty of time to come home on the coach with your husband."

"Well, then, I thank you kindly, Sir John, I'll go," she said. "Shure it will ever and always be a great thing for me to say I'm the first woman that ever drove from Drogheda to Dublin on the railroad."

We did not get in quite as soon as we expected, and by the time she arrived at the coach-office, in Dorset Street, Peter was already on the box, with the reins in his hand, ready to start. Great was his amazement to see her.

"What the divil brought you here?" he said.

"To go home on the coach with you, Peter dear," said she.

"How did you come up to town?"

"On the railroad with Sir John and Mr. Le Fanu," she said.

"Well, go back the way you came," said Peter, in a rage, "for the divil a step you shall come with me;" and off he drove.

No engine was going back to Drogheda that day, so she hired a car to drive the thirty miles, for which her husband, of course, had to pay; but that wasn't all, for as Mrs. Pentlebury had a remarkably lively tongue of her own, he got a blowing up that he remembered till the day of his death. So poor Peter had cut off his nose to vex his face.

Some time after the railway from Dublin to Belfast was opened, before the days of smoking-carriages, I got into an empty compartment at

Scarva junction, and had just lit my cigar, when an old gentleman got in. I had to ask him whether he had any objection to smoking, and pending his answer I put my hand with my cigar in it out of the window. I felt the cigar hitting hard against something, and heard a voice crying out, "Well, if you wouldn't give me anything, you mightn't go dirtying my hand like that." It was a porter who had stretched his hand for an expected sixpence, instead of which the lighted end of my cigar was pressed into the palm of his hand.

Ilberry, formerly traffic superintendent of the Great Southern and Western Railway, told me of an incident which he saw occur about the same time. A man was sitting in a carriage next to the open window with his back towards the engine, in one hand a pipe, and in the other a match, which he was ready to light, though he was afraid to do so till the train should start, as he saw a porter watching him. Just as the train started he lit the pipe, put it in his mouth, stretched his head out of the window, and putting his thumb, with his fingers extended, to his nose, gave a farewell salute to the porter. He, however, had failed to perceive or reckon with another porter standing on the platform between him and the engine, who deftly plucked the pipe out of his mouth, put it in his own, and, with his thumb to his nose, returned the passenger's salute as the train moved off, leaving him, poor fellow, without his smoke or his pipe.

Father H—— told me that he had got into a second-class carriage one night by the last train leaving Dublin for Bray. Before the train started a woman, whose name he could not remember, but whom he recognized as a parishioner, came to the door and said, "Father James, have you any objection to my coming in here?" "Not the least," said he. So in she came, and sat on the seat opposite to him. Off went the train at such a pace as he had never known before; it jumped and swayed from side to side. Father H—— was naturally much alarmed. The woman, observing this, said to him, "Don't be the least unasy, Father James. Sure it's my Jim that's driving; and when he has a dhrop taken, it's him that can make her walk."

CHAPTER XV.

Tory Island : its king, customs, and captive—William Dargan : his career and achievements—Agricultural and industrial experiments—Bianconi, the carman—Sheridan Knowles: his absence of mind—Absent-minded gentlemen—Legal complications—Judges and barristers—Lord Norbury.

IT was when on an inspection for the Irish Light Board, upwards of thirty years ago, that I visited Tory Island, which lies well out in the Atlantic, some seven miles off the extreme north-west corner of Ireland. The cliffs, on the north of the island, are very fine; the south, where we landed, is flat. The islanders, with very few exceptions, spoke only Irish. Their carts had no wheels; they were what are called sleigh carts, the shafts being prolonged till they touched the ground, beyond which point they were turned up, and had a sort of creel laid on them, in which the load was carried. I was very anxious to see the famous king of Tory Island, of whom I had heard, a very diminutive man, almost a dwarf, but of much intelligence. I was, however, disappointed, as his Majesty was too drunk to give an audience to visitors. He had, for two days previously, been in bed in that condition. At the time of my visit the islanders were in much anxiety about their fuel, as their turf bog was all but exhausted, and after a year or two they would have no turf. I hear they now get coal by a steamer, on her voyage from the Clyde to Sligo. I was told that some of the priests who had been stationed on the island had, from utter loneliness, taken to imbibing poteen whisky a little too freely, thereby causing scandal, and that the bishop had, for a time at least, withdrawn the clergy from the island, leaving the inhabitants to make the most of the ministrations of the priest of the parish nearest to them on the mainland, who visited them from time to time as the weather permitted.

In the south and west of Ireland marriages amongst the peasantry, with rare exceptions, take place during Shrove-tide. Many of the people think it would not be lucky to be married at any other time of the year; consequently the priest always, when it was possible, visited the island during Shrove for the purpose of solemnizing any weddings which had been arranged. It, however, sometimes happened that the weather was so stormy for weeks together that no boat could approach the island, so it had been arranged that, when this occurred, the engaged couples should at an appointed hour assemble on the east shore of the island, while the priest, standing on the shore of the mainland opposite to them, read the marriage ceremony across the water. As soon as the storm abated he went to the island and did whatever more was necessary to render the marriages valid in the eye of the law and of the Church. I cannot vouch for the truth of this, though I heard it from a very trustworthy man. He said the young people were not considered really married till after the visit of the priest; but that they liked to be, at all events, partly married before Shrove was over.

The following occurrence I know took place, not more than eight years ago. A boat, rowed by some Tory islanders, arrived at Gweedore, which is about sixteen miles from the island, in quest of a doctor, whom they found and brought back with them to Tory. His help was wanted for one of the chief men there, who was very ill. The doctor's people expected him home that evening or, at latest, next morning; but for five days he never appeared. His friends and patients grew uneasy about him; they knew it was not the weather that kept him from returning, for it happened to be particularly fine; so a friend of mine, and some others, rowed off to Tory Island to seek for him. There they found him a prisoner. It appears that immediately after his visit the sick man began to amend, and next morning was very nearly well; but the islanders were so delighted and charmed with the doctor and with his wonderful skill, that they determined to keep him permanently with them. They lodged him in their best house, gave him the best food they had, with whisky unlimited; and nothing he could say would induce them to take him back to Gweedore. His friends, however, rescued him and brought him safely home.

In the course of my work as an engineer, amongst others I made two friends, both long since dead, of whom I think I may here say a few words. They were both remarkable men; both self-made men. The one was William Dargan, the great Irish railway contractor; the other the well-known coach and car proprietor, Charles Bianconi.

Dargan was the son of a tenant farmer, in the county of Carlow. At a school near his house he received a sound elementary education, and from early years showed special aptitude for figures. After leaving school he obtained a subordinate appointment—that of timekeeper, if I remember rightly—on the great Holyhead Road, under Telford, the engineer. His intelligence, and the trust which he inspired, so pleased Telford that a few years later, when the new mail-coach road was about to be made from Dublin to Howth Harbour, from whence the packets carrying the mails for London were to start, he entrusted to Dargan the superintendence of the work. So satisfactory was his performance of his duties that, on the completion of the road, the Treasury granted him a gratuity of three hundred pounds in addition to his salary. This was the capital upon which he commenced his career as a contractor. His first, or almost his first, contract was for an embankment on the river Shannon, near Limerick, in which Lord Monteagle and Sir Matthew Barrington were interested; and so struck were they with the manner in which he carried out the work, and the straightforwardness with which he settled his accounts, that they became through life his fast friends. His first large undertaking was the construction of the railway from Dublin to Kingstown, which was begun in 1831, and was the first passenger railway made in Ireland, and the second in the Three Kingdoms. From this time forward he found no difficulty in obtaining large contracts in every part of Ireland. He had two, amounting together to over a million sterling, with the Great Southern and Western Railway Company and the Midland Company; and others which in those days were considered large, with most of the other railway companies in Ireland. I have settled as engineer for different companies many of his accounts, involving many hundred thousand pounds. His thorough honesty, his willingness to yield a disputed point, and his wonderful rapidity of decision, rendered it a pleasure, instead of a trouble, as it generally is, to settle these accounts; indeed, in my life I have never met a man more quick in intelligence, more clear sighted, and more thoroughly honourable.

By the year 1849 he had amassed a large fortune, and he at once turned his attention to the manner in which he could best apply it in benefiting his country. The first project which suggested itself to him was to introduce into the south of Ireland the culture of flax, which had rendered the north so prosperous. He took a large farm near Kildinan, some ten miles north of Cork, which he at once laid out for flax cultivation, and on which he erected scutch mills. He then offered to supply all the farmers through that part of the country with flax seed at his own expense, and to purchase their crops from them at the current market price in Belfast, and this he undertook to do for at least two years. Very few farmers, however, accepted his offer and made the experiment even in the first year, and scarcely any in the second, and the project became a total failure. It is difficult to understand why this should have been so, unless it was due to the fear that the flax crop might exhaust the land, and to the inveterate dislike of the southern farmers to try any new experiment; for it is with them a fixed conviction that it is best for them to go on, as they themselves express it, " as we did ever and always."

There was nothing in the soil or climate to prevent the successful cultivation of flax, for though its growth in the south of Ireland had altogether ceased for many years, yet I can remember the time when every farmer, no matter how small his holding, had a plot of flax, from which all the linen required for his household was manufactured, the spinning being done by his wife and daughters, and the weaving by the local weavers, of whom there were then numbers in every part of the country.

Dargan's next project for his country's good was a thoroughly successful one. It was the great Industrial Exhibition in Dublin in the year 1853, all expenses in connection with which, including the erection of the building itself, were defrayed by him. It was opened by her Majesty the Queen and the Prince Consort, who came to Ireland expressly for the purpose. They did Dargan the honour of visiting him and Mrs. Dargan at his beautiful residence, Mount Anville, a few miles from Dublin. Her Majesty wished him to accept a baronetcy, which he declined, at the same time expressing his gratitude for this mark of her Majesty's approval. The Queen then announced to him her intention to present him with a bust of herself, and also one of the Prince Consort; and, with her usual thoughtful kindness, desired that he should select the sculptor by whom they were to be executed. He, from his friendship for the man, selected Johnny Jones, of whom I have already said much.

His next project was the establishment of a great thread factory at Chapelizod, near Dublin, where he purchased, and added to, large mill premises, and, at great expense, fitted them with all the necessary machinery. It may have been that the demand for thread was sufficiently supplied by the English manufacturers; but whether it was from this or from other causes, the undertaking completely failed.

After this Dargan, unfortunately for himself, threw all his energies into the Dublin, Wicklow, and

Wexford Railway, in which he invested nearly his whole fortune, and of which he became chairman. In connection with this line he spent large sums on the improvement of Bray, the now well-known watering-place on the coast about midway between Dublin and Wicklow. He built the Turkish baths (now the assembly rooms) at a cost of £8000, and also a handsome terrace. He made the esplanade, which has since been secured by a sea-wall and much improved by the energetic town commissioners. He also aided largely in providing first-rate hotel accommodation there. This expenditure, though large, would not have seriously impaired his means had the railway proved as successful as he hoped it would have done; but the great depression in railway property, which began about that time, so lowered the value of all his investments that they for a time became of little worth; and this remarkable man (for a remarkable man he was) a few years later died comparatively poor, and, to use his own words, "of a broken heart."

I had almost forgotten to mention two of his favourite maxims. These were, "A spoonful of honey will catch more flies than a gallon of vinegar," and "Never show your teeth unless you can bite." On these, as he himself often told me, he had acted from early years, and it was to them that he attributed much of his success in life.

There is a statue of Dargan by Johnny Jones in front of the National Gallery in Dublin.

Charles Bianconi, a native of Tregolo, a village in the Duchy of Milan, arrived in Ireland in 1802, at the age of fifteen, as an apprentice, with other Italian boys, to one Andrea Faroni, a dealer in prints and statuettes. These boys were employed in travelling about the country selling their master's wares, Bianconi's district lying principally in the counties of Wexford and Waterford. After about two years he left Faroni and started a similar business on his own account. In 1806 he settled in Carrick-on-Suir, in the county of Tipperary, and in the following year he went to Clonmel.

In his many journeys from town to town he often felt the want of any means of conveyance for travellers, the only public vehicles of any kind being the few mail and stage coaches on the main roads. In 1815 Bianconi started a one-horse stage car, carrying six passengers, between Clonmel and Cahir; and the experiment was so successful that before the end of the year he had several similar cars plying between different towns in Tipperary and Waterford. This business prospered to such an extent that by the year 1843 his cars—many of them carrying twenty passengers and drawn by four horses—were plying from market town to market town over the whole south and west of Ireland and a considerable portion of the north. It was on some journey on one of these cars that I first made his acquaintance.

They were well known throughout Ireland as

Bianconi's cars, and even after the development of railways he still ran his cars and various coaches to the different railway termini. At one time his vehicles were performing journeys daily of over four thousand miles in twenty-two different counties, and he used to frequently boast, to the credit of the peasantry, that no injury whatever had been done to any of his property in all these districts.

I met him often afterwards, and had many opportunities of noticing the quick intelligence which had led to his success. But with all his cleverness he combined a kindness and simplicity of character rarely met with. He realized a fortune, and purchased an estate on the banks of the Suir, in the county of Tipperary. I have often heard him talk of the struggles of his early days; and he used to delight in showing to his guests the pack which he had carried when selling his wares as a boy. The following is a characteristic letter, written in his eighty-first year, and the last I ever had from him :—

"Longfield, 10. 10. '69.

"MY DEAR SIR,

"I learn with great pleasure your being in the country, and if you condescend to visit *a carman's stage*, I will drive you from this to Ballygriffin (five miles), where the late Sir Thomas Fitzgerald, pending his father's lifetime, supported himself and his large family on the salmon he caught in that beautiful spot, and which is strictly preserved by yours

"Very truly,
"CHARLES BIANCONI.

"W. R. Le Fanu, Esq.

"And we will bring Morgan John O'Connell, who is at present at home, with us."

Another friend of mine, of whom I saw a good deal at this time, was Sheridan Knowles, the dramatist. He was one of the most absent-minded I ever knew. Mrs. Norton and her sister, Lady Dufferin, were engaged to dine with him, and he was in the evening to read aloud to them one of his plays, which he had just finished. When the day came Knowles forgot all about it, dined early with his family, as his custom was, and was just sitting down to tea at eight o'clock when his two guests arrived. He was so much put out that he did not know what to say or do; but they were so pleasant and so full of fun, that they soon put him at his ease. They protested that they much preferred tea to dinner, and before they went praised his play so much that he was as happy as a king.

Some time afterwards a still more awkward incident occurred. He was walking down Regent Street with a friend, when a gentleman stopped him and said—

"You're a pretty fellow, Knowles."

"Why? What have I done?" said Knowles.

"Only kept us waiting dinner on Wednesday from half-past seven till eight, and never came."

"Good heavens!" said Knowles; "I forgot all about it. Ah, my dear fellow, can you ever forgive me?"

"I can and will," said the other, "on one condition—that you dine with me at half-past seven next Wednesday."

"Thank you, my dear friend; I shall be delighted."

"Don't forget—half-past seven, Wednesday. Good-bye," said the gentleman, and off he went.

Knowles, in much excitement, turned to his friend and said, "Isn't this absence of mind a dreadful calamity? Just think of my having kept that dear fellow and his family waiting for me in that way! By-the-by, do you know who he was?"

"No," said his friend.

"By Jove, no more do I!" said Knowles, and ran after the man as fast as he could go. But he had gone so far that Knowles could neither see nor catch him.

At one time he went on the stage, and used to act in his own plays—*Virginius*, *William Tell*, and *The Hunchback*. One night, when he was to act *The Hunchback* in Dublin, I went into his dressing-room at the Theatre Royal, and found him in a state of great agitation.

"Look at me, William—look at me," said he, stretching out his right leg, on which was a red stocking—the other leg was bare.

"What is the matter?" I said.

"Ah," said he, "isn't an actor's a fearful life? The other stocking is lost. The overture has begun. I must put on black stockings, and in five minutes go on the stage to disgrace myself. The part was never acted in black stockings. Oh! like a dear fellow, pull off this red one."

This I did, and under it was the lost one. He had put the two on one leg!

One evening I heard his daughters say to him that they were sure that a Mr. H——, who was a constant visitor at the house, had false whiskers. Knowles was indignant, and said that H—— was above any such nonsense as that. Half an hour later H—— came in. Knowles at once went up to him and said, "My dear boy, these girls of mine have been taking away your character. They say that these are false." As he said this he took hold of one of H——'s whiskers, which came off in his hand. The girls flew from the room, leaving their father to explain as best he could.

Another absent-minded man was one of the Battersbys, of the county of Meath. On a very wet day he came into my office, and, as he was going, put on his hat and took his umbrella in his hand. My hat and umbrella were on a table near the door. As he said good-bye to me he took up my umbrella, and was going off with an umbrella in each hand. "Wet as it is," I said, "won't you find two umbrellas rather too much?" "A thousand pardons," he said. "I'm always doing these absent sort of things." He put down my umbrella and took up my hat, and was walking off with two hats, one on his head, the other in his hand. I said, "I'm afraid you'll find two hats as inconvenient as two umbrellas."

But more absent-minded than either he or

Knowles was a Mr. Shaw of the post-office department in Edinburgh, who, as Professor Rankin told me, sometimes forgot his own name. One day, as he was on his way to visit Smith of Deanstone, he met a man who he thought was an acquaintance of his, and put out his hand to shake hands with him.

"I do not think, sir," said the man, "I have the honour of your acquaintance."

"Oh, indeed you have," said Shaw. "Don't you know me? I'm Smith of Deanstone."

"Then, sir," said the other, "I do not know you."

Shaw had not gone many paces, when it flashed across his mind that he had said the wrong name. He ran after the man, overtook him, and, giving him a slap on the back, said, "What an ass I am! I'm not Smith of Deanstone; I'm Shaw of the post-office."

"I don't care a d———n who you are, sir; but I wish you'd let me alone," said the other.

An intimate friend of Knowles was Young, the well-known actor. We went to see him taking his farewell of the Dublin audience. It was said that the reason for his retirement was that he had married a rich widow—a Mrs. Winterbottom—whose name he was reported to have taken. On this farewell night he was acting his favourite part, "Zanga," in *The Revenge*. His opening speech began in this way: "'Tis twice ten years since that great man—great let me call him, for he conquered me—made me the prisoner of his arm in fight. He slew my father and threw chains o'er me. I then was young." Here he was interrupted by a voice from the gallery crying out, "And now you're Winterbottom." I do not think he, in fact, took the name, for I met him years after still "Young."

Once I heard an amusing mistake in a name. As I walked up Whitehall with Sir Matthew Barrington and a Mr. Jeffers, Fonblanque passed by and nodded to me. "Do you know who that was?" said Sir Matthew to Jeffers. "No," said Jeffers. "Who was he?" "A remarkable man," said Sir Matthew. "That is Blanc-mange of the *Examiner.*" "No, no," said I—"Fonblanque." "Oh, of course!" said Sir M.; "but I never can remember names."

The well-known Irish judge, the late Judge B——, was neither absent-minded nor forgetful of names, but had a peculiarity of his own: this was that he constantly misunderstood, or pretended to misunderstand, what witnesses examined before him said. Many are the stories told of him, amongst others the following :—

At the Kildare Assizes at Naas a serious assault case was tried. Two men had quarrelled in a hayfield, where they were mowing, and one of them had nearly killed the other. A witness was asked how the quarrel began. He said that Cassidy had called Murphy a liar, and that then Murphy hit Cassidy with a scythe-board.

"Stop a moment; let me understand," said the judge. "Did Murphy lift up a sideboard and hit Cassidy with it?"

Witness. "He did, my lord."

Judge. "How did it happen that there was a sideboard out in the field?"

Witness. "We does always have them there, my lord, when we do be mowing."

Judge. "For what purpose?"

Witness. "To sharpen our scythes, my lord."

Counsel then, with some difficulty, made the judge understand that the witness meant a scythe-board, and not a sideboard.

Another case was one in which a man was indicted for robbery at the house of a poor widow. The first witness was her young daughter, who identified the prisoner as the man who had come into the house and broken her mother's chest.

Judge. "Do you say that the prisoner at the bar broke your mother's chest?"

Witness. "He did, my lord. He jumped on it till he smashed it entirely."

Judge (to Counsel). "How is this? Why is not the prisoner indicted for murder? If he smashed this poor woman's chest, in the way the witness has described, he must surely have killed her."

Counsel. "My lord, it was a wooden chest."

In the north of Ireland the peasantry pronounce the word witness "wetness." At Derry Assizes a man said he had brought his "wetness" with him to corroborate his evidence.

"Bless me," said the judge, "about what age are you?"

Witness. "Forty-two my last birthday, my lord."

Judge. "Do you mean to tell the jury that at that age you still have a wet nurse?"

Witness. "Of course I have, my lord."

Counsel hereupon interposed and explained.

Another case was also in the north, where "mill" is often pronounced "mull." The point at issue was whether a mill had been burned accidentally or maliciously. Dowse (afterwards Baron Dowse), as counsel for the miller, was trying to show that it must have been burnt maliciously, and that the contention of the opposite side, that it was an accident caused by the machinery becoming over-heated, was untenable. He asked a witness whether he had happened to feel the gudgeons (part of the machinery) before he left the place.

Witness. "I did, sir."

Dowse. "In what state were they?"

Witness. "Perfectly cool."

Judge. "I want to understand, Mr. Dowse, what gudgeons are?"

Dowse. "Little fishes, my lord."

Judge. "Then of course they were cool."

Dowse (*to Witness*). "In what state were the premises and the machinery that evening when you left?"

Witness. "All the machinery was perfectly right and cool, and the whole mull was as right as a trivet."

Judge. "Stop a moment; this is the first time we

have heard of the mull. What is a mull, Mr. Dowse?"

Dowse. "What you are making of this case, my lord."

Perhaps the most remarkable of all the stories told of this judge is the following. At the assizes at Clonmel, several men were indicted for manslaughter. The evidence went to show that all the prisoners had been in the fight against the man who had been killed. A witness was asked whether he could swear that the prisoner, Pat Ryan, had done anything to the deceased man. "Yes," he said, "when poor Ned Sullivan was lying on the ground, welthering in his blood, Pat Ryan came up and gave him a wipe of a clay alpin on the back of his head." The prisoners were convicted, and heavy sentences passed on all except Pat Ryan, whom the judge addressed in these words—

"Your case, Patrick Ryan, the court has taken into its merciful consideration, for though you were one of the party engaged in this terrible affair in which Sullivan lost his life, it appears that towards the end of the fight you were moved with compassion, for it has been distinctly proved by one of the witnesses for the prosecution, that when the unfortunate man was lying on the ground, bleeding from his wounds, you came behind him and wiped his head with a clean napkin."

He would have proceeded to pass a much lighter

sentence on Ryan than he had passed on the others had he not been stopped by counsel, who explained to him that a clay alpin is a heavy loaded stick, and that the " wipe " which Ryan had given Sullivan with it was in all probability his death-blow.

Many are the stories I have heard of judges and barristers in former days. Though some of them are well known, I shall venture to give a few which may be new to my readers. One of the best was connected with a case tried (in Limerick, I think) before Chief Baron O'Grady. Bushe was making a speech for the defence, when an ass began to bray loudly outside the court. "Wait a moment," said the Chief Baron. "One at a time, Mr. Bushe, if you please." When O'Grady was charging the jury, the ass again began to bray, if possible more loudly than before. "I beg your pardon, my lord," said Bushe, " may I ask you to repeat your last words; there is such an echo in this court I did not quite catch them."

Of Lord Norbury, the hanging judge, it was said that he was only once in his life known to shed tears, and that was at the theatre, at *The Beggar's Opera*, when the reprieve arrives for Captain Macheath.

When the income tax was about to be extended to Ireland, John Ryan, reader to the Court of Chancery, a very stingy old gentleman, was very much excited about it. "But," said he to a friend, "how will they find out what my income is?" "You'll be put on your oath to declare it, Mr.

Ryan," said his friend. "Oh, will they leave it to my oath?" said Ryan, and walked off in high glee.

Witnesses try in various ways to avoid taking what they consider a binding oath. A favourite plan supposed to relieve them from all obligation is, when being sworn, to kiss the thumb instead of kissing the book. Before Baron Pennefather, at Tralee Assizes, a witness did so. One of the counsel said, "The witness kissed his thumb, my lord." "Why did the witness kiss his thumb?" asked the baron. "He is blind of an eye, my lord," replied Mr. Hurley, the clerk of the Crown.

CHAPTER XVI.

Irish bulls—Sayings of Sir Boyle Roche—Plutarch's lives—A Grand Jury's decision—Clerical anecdotes and Biblical difficulties—A harmless lunatic—Dangerous recruits—Tom Burke—Some memorials to the Board of Works.

OF Irish bulls there is no end. Some have become household words, as, for example, Sir Boyle Roche's: "A man couldn't be in two places at once, barring he was a bird." There are others of his not so well known.

In the Irish House of Commons in 1795, during a debate on the leather tax, the Chancellor of the Exchequer, Sir John Parnell, observed "that in the prosecution of the present war, every man ought to be ready to give his last guinea to protect the remainder."

Mr. Vandeleur said that "however that might be, a tax on leather would press heavily on the barefooted peasantry of Ireland." To which Sir Boyle Roche replied that this could be easily removed by making the under leathers of wood.

In speaking in favour of the Union, he said that one of its effects would be "that the barren hills would become fertile valleys."

In another debate he said, "I boldly answer in the affirmative—no!"

In mentioning the Cape, he said that "myrtles were so common there, that they made birch brooms of them."

I am not sure whether it was he who in one of his speeches said, "You should refrain from throwing open the flood-gates of democracy lest you should pave the way for a general conflagration."

He once mentioned some people who "were living from hand to mouth like the birds of the air."

Sir Richard Steele, another well-known Irishman, was asked by an English friend how it was that Irishmen were so remarkable for making bulls. "I believe," said he, "it is something in the air of the country; and I dare say if an Englishman was born here, he would do the same."

Tom Moore used to tell a story that when he was staying, as a boy, with an uncle at Sandymount, as they walked into Dublin early one morning, they found a dead highwayman lying on the road, who had evidently been shot during the night by some one whom he had attacked. There was a small bullet-hole in his right temple. An old woman was looking at him. "Gentlemen," said she, "isn't it the blessing of God it didn't hit him in the eye?" This is mentioned in some life of Moore.

Some people were laughing at an Irishman who won a race for saying, " Well, I'm first at last." "You needn't laugh," said he; "sure, wasn't I behind before?"

The following conversation was heard in the Fenian times some years ago:—

Tom. "These are terrible times, Bill."

Bill. "Bedad, they are, Tom; it's a wondher if we'll get out of the world alive."

Tom. "I'm afeard we won't, even if we had as many lives as Plutarch."

Bill. "If Oliver Cromwell could only come up out of hell, he'd soon settle it."

Tom. "Bedad, maybe he'd rather stop where he is."

In the coffee-room at an hotel in Dublin an Irish gentleman said to a friend who was breakfasting with him, "I'm sure that is my old college friend West at that table over there." "Then why don't you go over and speak to him?" said his friend. "I'm afraid to," said the other; "for he is so very shy, that he would feel quite awkward if it wasn't he."

It was Caulfield, an Irishman who succeeded Marshall Wade as manager of roads in Scotland, who wrote and posted up in the Highlands the famous lines—

"Had you seen these roads before they were made,
You'd lift up your hands and bless Marshall Wade."

About seventy years ago the Grand Jury of the county of Tipperary passed the following resolutions:—

" 1st. That a new court house shall be built.

" 2nd. That the materials of the old court house be used in building the new court house.

" 3rd. That the old court house shall not be taken down till the new court house is finished."

Here is a bull, or rather a mixed metaphor, which appeared in an English newspaper. In a leading article in the *Morning Post*, in 1812, occurs the following passage:—" We congratulate ourselves most on having torn off Cobbett's mask, and revealed his cloven foot. It was high time that the hydra head of faction should be soundly rapped over the knuckles."

It was a Scotchman—Professor Wilkie, I think—who said to a boy whom he met, "I was sorry to hear that there was fever in your family last spring. Was it you or your brother that died of it?" "It was me, sir," said the boy.

A barrister defending a prisoner in Limerick said, "Gentlemen of the jury, think of his poor mother—his only mother."

The following was told me many years ago. Some young fellows in the navy shaved the head of a brother officer, an Irishman, when he was drunk, and put him to bed. He had previously given orders that he was to be called at five in the morning, and was accordingly called at that hour. When he looked in the glass and saw an appearance so unlike what he expected, "Hang me," said he, "if they haven't called the wrong man!"

The present County Surveyor of Cork, Mr. Kirkby, is a graduate of Cambridge, and sometimes writes " M.A. Cantab" after his name. At Road Sessions a ratepayer said to another, " That Mr. Kirkby must be a very clever chap, for sure he is a Cantab of Oxford."

A neighbour of mine said that a very fine horse he had bought a few days previously had gone lame. " What is the matter with him?" asked a Mr. T——. " I am greatly afraid he has got the vernacular," said he (of course he meant navicular). " Dear me!" said T——, " I never heard of any quadruped having that disease, except Balaam's ass."

As I have given some stories of the Bench and Bar, it would be scarcely fair to ignore the Church, so I shall insert a few anecdotes of clergymen.

My father, arrayed in knee-breeches, shovel hat, and apron, was walking home in a hard frost one Sunday afternoon from the Chapel Royal, at Dublin Castle, where he had preached. As he went along the footway round St. Stephen's Green, where in frosty weather boys always make slides, he accidentally got on one, slid along it, and came down on his knees, bursting his inexpressibles. An old woman who was passing addressed him in these words: " Isn't it a shame for you, you old blackguard, to be making slides to knock decent people down? It's what you ought to be tuck up by the police."

I told this story to Thackeray, and shortly

afterwards saw a little drawing in *Punch* illustrating it.

Many years ago, in St. Catherine's Church, in Dublin, I heard a sermon preached by a Mr. Coghlan, a queer-looking, fat old man, with a very round red face, and snow-white hair. He had been speaking on the virtue of charity, and ended his discourse thus: "And now I implore each one of you to put to himself or herself this vital question, 'Am I in love?'" then, after a pause, and turning to the right, "Am I in love?" then turning to the left, "Am I in love—and charity with all men?" But before he came to "charity with all men" there went a very audible titter through the congregation.

Of the same sort was the sermon of an old gentleman, formerly curate of St. Mark's parish in Dublin. He was preaching on the final separation of the bad from the good, and had taken for his text, "He shall set the sheep on His right hand, the goats on the left." He finished his sermon in the following words: "And now, my beloved brethren, I beseech each and every one of you, rich and poor, young and old, man and woman, before you go to bed this night, to put to yourselves this all-important question, 'Am I a sheep, or am I a goat?'"

My friend, the Rev. W. F. Boyle, told me that when speaking to a boy, whom he found herding pigs in a field, on the impropriety of never attending Sunday school, he waxed quite eloquent in his admonitions, and thought from the earnest look in the boy's eyes that he had made a deep impression. He paused for a reply, when the boy said, " Well, your raverence, pigs is the divil for rootin'." The earnest look, which Boyle had mistaken for attention to his advice, was in reality fixed on some of his pigs which were rooting in a far-off corner of the field.

Something of the same kind happened to the late Cardinal Cullen, who, when taking a walk by himself in the country one Sunday afternoon, saw a boy in a field holding a goat by a rope, when the following dialogue took place :—

Cardinal. " Were you at Mass to-day, my boy ? "
Boy. " No, I wasn't."
Cardinal. " Why not ? "
Boy. " I was houlding the goat."
Cardinal. " Were you at Mass last Sunday ? "
Boy. " No, I wasn't."
Cardinal. " Do you ever go to Mass at all ? "
Boy. " No, I don't. Don't I tell you I do be houlding the goat."
Cardinal. " But couldn't you sometimes get some one else to hold it ? "
Boy. " No, I couldn't. You don't know that goat. The divil couldn't hould that goat; you couldn't hould that goat yourself."

A clergyman in the county of Clare, much given to drawing the long bow, had quarrelled with the squire of the parish, on whose land was the best well in the country. One very dry summer, fifty years ago, all the other streams and wells in that part of the country were dried up, and the poor clergyman could get water nowhere, and said to a friend, "You can fancy the straits I am put to; last Sunday morning I had to shave with sherry."

The late Archdeacon Russell had a very noisy servant, whom he was obliged often to correct for the noise she made at her work. Very early one morning, as he was coming downstairs, there was a great clattering in the drawing-room, and he heard the servant saying, "Bad luck to you! you're the noisiest fire-irons I ever handled."

A strange parson, officiating in a country church in the absence of the rector, to his horror saw the gentleman who had handed the plate, when returning it to him, slip a half-crown off and put it into his waistcoat pocket. Immediately after the service he told the sexton to request the gentleman to come to him in the vestry room. When he came he said to him, " Sir, I never was so shocked and pained in my life. I distinctly saw you, sir, abstract a half-crown from the plate and put it into your pocket." " Of course you did," replied the man; " here it is. I always do so. You see when I get the plate, before I begin to hand it round, I always place a half-crown on it, in order to induce people to give more than they otherwise would, and I afterwards remove it as you saw me do."

When I was a boy I recollect my father coming home and telling us of an old lady he had been visiting, who, just as he came into the room, stirred the fire, by which she was sitting, and sent a cloud of sparks up the chimney. "Ay, ay," she said, "'man is born unto trouble, as the sparks fly upwards;' though indeed, sir, I never could see what trouble the sparks have in flying upwards."

I am not sure whether it was the same lady who asked a clergyman how it was that Solomon was permitted to have seven hundred wives, not to mention the three hundred other ladies. He explained to her that the manners and customs of those times were quite different from those of the present day. "Dear me," she said, "what privileges those early Christians had!"

There was an old blind lady in Dublin who used to have a little girl to read aloud to her. She was reading that part of the Book of Exodus where the building of the tabernacle is described. In reading the verse which says the roof is to be covered with badger's skins, the girl read aloud, "And a covering of beggar's skins." "What did you say, child?" said the old lady. "Beggar's skins, ma'am," said the girl. "Oh dear! oh dear!" said the old lady, "weren't those terrible times when it was just 'up with the beggar and off with his skin'!"

There are many stories of the witty priests in old times; I shall only mention two.

A farmer asked the well-known Father Tom Maguire what a miracle was. He gave him a very full explanation, which, however, did not seem quite to satisfy the farmer, who said—

"Now, do you think, your raverence, you could give me an example of miracles?"

"Well," said Father Tom, "walk on before me, and I'll see what I can do."

As he did so he gave him a tremendous kick behind.

"Did you feel that?" he asked.

"Why wouldn't I feel it?" said the farmer, rubbing the damaged place. "Begorra, I did feel it, sure enough."

"Well," said Father Tom, "it would be a miracle if you didn't."

Curran said to Father O'Leary (the wittiest priest of his day), "I wish you were St. Peter." "Why?" asked O'Leary. "Because," said Curran, "you would have the keys of heaven, and could let me in." "It would be better for you," said O'Leary, "that I had the keys of the other place, for then I could let you out."

In catechising a little girl the clergyman asked her, "What is the outward and visible sign in baptism?" "The babby, please, sir," said she.

Another on being asked what an epistle was, said, "The feminine of an apostle."

A short time ago a lady told me that in examining her class of boys in Bray, she asked one of them what John the Baptist meant by "fruits meet for repentance." He answered, "Apples and nuts, hams, gams, and pigs' cheeks." She was angry with him, thinking he was making fun; but on questioning him she found he was quite serious, and thought that the Baptist meant that they were to bring him fruits and meat to show their repentance (as he was rather tired of locusts and wild honey), and the fruits and meats best known to the boy were those he mentioned.

A clergyman explaining to some boys the passage in Scripture, "It is easier for a camel to go through the eye of a needle than for a rich man to enter into the kingdom of God," told them that this very strong expression was meant to show extreme difficulty, "for you know it would be quite impossible for a camel to go through the eye of a needle." "Of course it would, sir, on account of its humps," said one of the boys.

In connection with the Board of Works I held the office of Commissioner of Control of Lunatic Asylums in Ireland. On my first visit to Mullingar Asylum I was accompanied by Doctor Nugent (now Sir John Nugent), also a commissioner. As we went through the house, with the resident doctor, we saw in the day room, amongst other patients, a pleasing looking elderly man, on each of whose legs was a hay rope wound above, below, and round the knee. On our entering the room he said—

"Gentlemen, I understand you are here on behalf of the Government. If so, I have a very serious complaint to make."

We asked him what it was.

"It is," said he, "that for the last three days I have had nothing to eat."

The doctor called up the principal attendant, a large, fresh-looking young man. We asked him whether this was true.

"No," he said; "the gentleman gets as much as any one in the house, and has a great appetite."

"Gentlemen," said our friend, "I admit that I have a good appetite; but it is worse than useless to me, while this chubby, rosy-cheeked rascal eats everything I am supposed to get. Just look at him, gentlemen; see how fat he is growing on my food."

"Well," said the doctor, "come to tea with me this evening, and you shall have plenty of tea and cake and bread and butter."

"Are you in earnest, doctor?" said he.

"I am, indeed," said the doctor.

"Then, gentlemen," said our friend, "I have much pleasure in withdrawing the charge I have made."

The poor man had been a Roman Catholic priest, and was continually at his devotions, and tied the hay ropes (*suggauns*) round his legs, to save his trousers from being worn out by the constant kneeling. He was perfectly harmless, and before the following Christmas was allowed out of the asylum to live with his brother, who held a large farm, and who had, amongst other things, a peculiar and valuable breed of turkeys, of which he was proud. He had twenty-two of them, and on Christmas morning, on going into the fowl-house, he found every one of them dead. On inquiry, his brother confessed that he had got up very early in the morning and cut off their heads, as he thought they were to be cooked for the Christmas dinner. He had no opportunity of doing further damage on the farm, as he was at once sent back to the asylum.

The following I heard from Sir John Nugent. During the Crimean War a considerable sum as bounty was given to recruits on enlisting. A recruiting sergeant one morning enlisted two men in Queen Street in Dublin, gave them their bounty, and repaired with them to the Royal Oak public-house on the Quays, where they spent their money like men, drinking, and treating every soldier who came in. In the afternoon, when all the bounty was expended, the sergeant told them that they were now to go with him to the Royal Barracks.

"But," said one of them, "maybe you don't know what we are."

"Come along," said the sergeant. "What does it matter what you were? You are soldiers now."

"But," said the other, "maybe you don't know that we are lunatics—and dangerous lunatics, too. We got out of Richmond Asylum last night."

The sergeant did not believe them, and a row had begun, when the police came in and interposed, and persuaded the sergeant to take them up to the asylum and test the truth of what they had said. So up they went, and great was the joy of the officials there when they appeared, for they were indeed dangerous lunatics who had escaped.

Amongst a few perquisites which the Commissioners of Public Works in Ireland enjoy are a buck and a doe every year from the royal herd in the Phœnix Park. I had written some years ago to the deer-keeper to send me my buck on the following Tuesday. On that morning, as I was dressing, my servant came to my room and said—

"The man is below, sir, with a haunch of venison."

"Go down," I said, "and see whether he has all the venison."

He returned saying that the man had got only the haunch.

"Go down and tell him to go back at once for the rest of the animal, and say that I am greatly annoyed at having been sent only a haunch."

He returned with the haunch in his hand, saying, "The man says, sir, that that was all he was told to leave."

I looked at the label on the venison, and found it was a present from Lord Powerscourt. I ran downstairs as fast as I could to try to catch the messenger. Luckily he had not gone. I endeavoured to explain the mistake I had made. He did not seem quite to take it in, for he said—

"I have another haunch, sir, but I was told to leave it at Mr. Brewster's; but, if you think his lordship won't be displeased, I'll leave it with your honour, if you think you ought to have it."

The following letter, which shows the confidence Galway men have in each other, is perhaps worth inserting here. I received it from the late Tom Burke, then Under-Secretary for Ireland, with a note to say that he had referred the writer to us, as we, and not he, had the entire control over the deer in the Phœnix Park. For obvious reasons I have omitted the address.

"............,
"December 18, 1879.

"DEAR SIR,
"Will you kindly excuse me as a Galway man, acquainted with a few, at least, of your friends, if I trouble you by inquiring how I could procure a small bit of venison against Christmas Day. I understand the matter is very easy to those who have either friends or acquaintances in the park; but though I cannot presume to count you amongst either, still as a namesake and a native of the same county I make bold to write you what otherwise would be a very presumptuous letter.

"I could easily send for the venison if I knew where to get it.

"Pray excuse my novel request.
"Your obedient servt,
"ROBT. BURKE.

"Right Hon. T. H. Burke."

Tom Burke was a very old and dear friend of mine, and was one of a little club of twelve members who for some years dined once a month at each other's houses, and among whom were my brother and myself. I never can forget my grief and horror when on Sunday morning, the 7th of May, 1882, the sergeant of police in Enniskerry came to my house and told me that he and Lord Frederick Cavendish had on the previous evening been murdered in the Phœnix Park. I felt it all the more as I had been talking to them both but a few hours before their death. From Lord Frederick I had received much kindness while he was Financial Secretary to the Treasury, and I had hoped to see much of him as Chief Secretary here.

Our secretary often got amusing letters, particularly from farmers who were borrowers under the Land Improvement Acts. Here is one which came from a man who had been refused a second instalment of a loan because he had misapplied the first.

"SIR,
"I spent the money all right; send me the rest, and don't be humboling me any more. Send it at once, I tell ye. Hell to your souls! send me my money, or I'll write to Mr. Parnell about it.
"Yours affectionately,
"JAMES RYAN.

I suppose most of the letters Ryan received were from relations in America, and seeing that they said "affectionately," he thought that was the correct word to use.

Another from a man in like circumstances was as follows:—

"HONOURED SIR,

"I send you these few lines, hoping that you are in the enjoyment of good health, as I am, thanks be to God, at this present writing. I write also to let you know that you are a disgrace to common society, and that you had better send me the money you owe me at once, or you'll hear more about it.

"Yours, honoured sir,
"DAVID CARROLL."

Here is one other. It is from a small farmer, who had in his hands the balance of a loan (£8), which he would neither expend nor refund. After many fruitless endeavours to make him do one or the other, a peremptory letter was sent to him, saying that if he did not within a week repay the amount, the Board's solicitor would be directed to take proceedings at once against him for its recovery. He replied as follows:—

"MY DEAR SECRETARY AND GENTLEMEN OF THE HONORABLE BOARD OF WORKS,

"Asking me to give back £8 is just like asking a beautiful and healthy young lady for a divorce, and she in the oughtmost love with her husband, as I am with each and every one of ye.

"I am, your sincere friend,
"JAMES CLARKE."

The enforcement of the fishery laws in Ireland was, some years ago, one of the duties of our Board. We constantly received memorials from people summoned for, or convicted of, breaches of those laws. The following is one of them:—

A HUMBLE PETITION. 241

"Balinamana West, Sept. 19, 1869.

"*To ye most worship Gentlemen Commisioners of the Public Works of Ireland.*

"THE MEMORIAL OF THOMAS AND ANN EGAN AND MARGRET EGAN

"Most humbly showeth, my lords, that this memorialist states to your worships that on the shore of Balinamana west leading with the public oyster bank Thomas Egan left few hundred oysters steeping on the lower shower last season, and could not lift them until the season was out. The water Bailiff passed by and found few small oysters close there which he summoned to oranmore Petty Sessions. his two little daughters was seeking for some cockels along the shore which he says found few small oysters with them which he summoned also. The court will open on thursday next. this memorialist begs to take leave to your worships most presious time hoping as they are most distressed creatures and a father of 12 in a weak family of helpless children and innocent of any charge and was not aware of any by-law act they confidently and most humbly crave and implore your worship will order them to be acquited of the first charge of the kind or to be imprisonment will be leyd on them, as they are distressed poor creatures could not aford to no fine for which they will as in duty ever pray."

The following story was told me by one of my colleagues at the Board of Works just before I retired, two years ago:—

An Irish gentleman whom he knew had a splendid-looking cow, but she kicked so much that it took a very long time and was nearly impossible to milk her; so he sent her to a fair to be sold, and told his herd to be sure not to sell her without letting the buyer know her faults. He brought home a large price, which he had got for her. His master was surprised, and said—

"Are you sure you told all about her?"

"Bedad, I did, sir!" said the herd. "He asked me whether she was a good milker? 'Begorra, sir,' says I, 'it's what you'd be tired milking her!'"

CHAPTER XVII.

Shooting and fishing—Good snipe grounds—Killarney and Powerscourt—My fishing record—Playing a rock—Salmon flies—Salmon and trout—Grattan's favourites—Hooking a bird—Fishing anecdotes—Lord Spencer's adventure.

SHOOTING and fishing have been my favourite sports. The former, in my early days, was with the old flint gun, which had been brought to great perfection. It was quite wonderful how few mis-fires one had. When these flint-locks had been made as perfect as possible, they were superseded by percussion guns, which in their turn gave place to breechloaders. So it is with almost everything. I have had much shooting of many sorts, but snipe shooting was my favourite; and many a good day I have had with the old flint gun. My best have been with a muzzleloader. I never was a very good shot, except at snipe and woodcock. At rabbits I was very bad, especially when they were crossing rides. I constantly shot behind them, and sympathized with the Frenchman who couldn't hit them, "Dey are so short." But at woodcock or snipe few men could beat me. I have shot as many as eighteen snipe in as many consecutive shots, and often from twelve to fourteen without a miss. Snipe shooting, alas! is not what it used to be. Drainage of marshes and fields has in some places abolished it, in others greatly injured it. There are few places now in Ireland where thirteen or fourteen couple would not be considered a good day, and on many lands where I have often shot from five and twenty to thirty couple a day one-third of the number could not now be found. Here are two of the best days I have ever had—I take them from my diary—

"*Dingle*, 12*th February*, 1855.—I shot Galorrus bog; bagged 48 couple of snipe, a mallard, 2 plover, and a curlew. Ran out of shot at 3 p.m."

"*Dingle*, 13*th February*, 1855.—I shot part of Cohen's bog; bagged 60 couple of snipe, a woodcock, a teal, a curlew, and a hare. I took out with me 2 lbs. of powder and 14 lbs. of shot, and had very little left in the evening."

On the same two days a cousin of mine who was with me killed forty-seven couple of snipe, four plover, a woodcock, and a teal.

As we sat at our dinner at the inn in Dingle, rejoicing over our good sport, we were attended by a very grumpy waiter, evidently from his rich Dublin brogue an importation from that city, sulky and dissatisfied with his lot. I happened to say to my cousin, "I think we are now nearly in the most westerly spot in Ireland." The waiter (it was the first time he had spoken except in monosyllables) said, " Yes, gentlemen, you are in the most westerly spot; and, what is more, you are in the most damnable spot in Ireland!" He then relapsed into sullen silence.

On Lord Carlisle's first visit to Galway, when he was Lord Lieutenant of Ireland, a waiter—something of the same sort as our friend—was told off specially to wait on him. On handing a dish of peas to him at dinner, he said, " Pays, yer Excellency;" then *sotto voce*, "and if I was you, the divil a one iv thim I'd touch, for the're as hard as bullets!"

These great days were on Lord Ventry's property, and I was glad to hear from him that these best of birds are still plentiful there. His son not very long ago shot over forty in a day.

The snipe shooting near Killarney was very good indeed, though not equal to that at Dingle. Lord Kenmare kindly gave me leave to shoot over all his property there, except the woods and coverts; so did Herbert of Muckross over all his, with the exception of one estate, which he preserved for himself and friends who might be staying with him at Muckross, though I fear it was sometimes visited by poachers from Killarney. As I was shooting on the adjoining estate, my attendant, one Callaghan McCarthy, said to me—

" Your honour might as well try that other bog beyant there."

"Callaghan," I said, "don't you know I have not leave from Mr. Herbert to shoot there?"

"What matter, your honour?" said he. "Sure you might as well shoot it as any other blackguard out of Killarney."

In the neighbourhood of Cork I have often in a day killed from twenty to thirty couple. Near Blarney, on the slope of a hill, there was a spring, surrounded by mosses and reeds, where in time of frost there were sure to be at least three or four snipe. Once before I got very near it one got up; he flew low and right away from me. 'Twas a long shot, too, and I missed him. I reloaded and walked on, expecting the others to get up, when lo! just by the spring were two, each with a wing broken, hopping about. I had chanced to hit them on the ground when firing at the other.

About twelve miles from Cork, in a bog near Castlemartyr (one of the best, but for its size, I ever shot), there is a similar spot. The late Cooper Penrose, to whom it belonged, told me that when he went to shoot there, before he went into the bog, he always fired at this spot, which was marked by red and yellow moss, and seldom failed to pick up from one to four snipe.

'Twas on this bog a sparrow-hawk swooped down and carried off a snipe I had wounded.

At Hillville, some twenty miles west of Tralee, I have had some of my best days. Near there one evening, after a very hard day, during which I had bagged twenty-nine couple of snipe and a mallard, I sank nearly to my middle in a bog. I was very tired, and but for the help of the man who was carrying my game-bag I do not think I could have pulled myself out. I was nearly in as bad a plight as the gentleman about whom a girl called out to her father, "Oh, father, father! come out quick and help Mr. Neligan; he is up to his ankles in the bog!" "Well, Mary," said he, "what harm will that do him?" "Ah, but, father, sure his head is downwards!" said she.

For over forty years I have seen Killarney nearly every year, but never did I see it look so beautiful as on one cloudless winter day, when we were cock shooting in the woods on Toomey's mountain. The hills above and around us, all clad in snow, glistening in the sun; below us was the lake; every island, with its trees, reflected in the water, calm and clear as crystal; and the woods along its margin green as in summer, so full are they of arbutus and holly.

The following autumn I was shooting with my friend, the late John Pennefather, on Lord Glengal's part of the Galtees, where grouse are not plentiful. We were restricted to seven brace in the day; but they need not have restricted us, for after a long day, in which we had worked uncommonly hard, we had only six and a half brace. We were very anxious to get our other bird, but one dog had gone lame, and the other was so tired that he began to set larks and other small birds, as tired dogs will do.

At last, however, he came to a very steady set high above us on the hill.

"Come on," said Pennefather; "he has them at last."

"Go up yourself," I said; "it is only a lark, or something of the sort."

"Come on, lazy fellow, and we'll make the seven brace. Look now how steady he is!"

So with our weary legs up the weary way we trudged. As we got up to the dog a large yellow frog jumped from before his nose; nothing else was there; and we descended sadly.

My last day's shooting was at Powerscourt—a party of eighteen; we went up for a hare drive on Douce and the War Hill. I and the late Mr. Gray, the artist, were together. We climbed at such a pace that by the time we were halfway up the mountain, my heart was beating in a fearful way.

"I'll go no farther," said I to Gray; "I'll go back and shoot woodquests in Powerscourt."

"Come on, man, come on," said Gray; "you'll be all right in a minute."

"I can't," I said, "there are drums beating in my ears for the last ten minutes."

"Nonsense," said he. "There are cannons going off in my ears for twenty minutes. Let us sit down for five minutes and get our breath, and we'll be all right."

So we did, and got on well for the rest of the day. Our bag was 505 hares, and a good many grouse; but the marching up the mountains, with young fellows, at four miles an hour was, at my age, too much for me; so I gave up shooting.

Not so with fishing, about which I am as keen as ever; and last summer, in my seventy-seventh year, I killed 54 salmon and peel; 128 sea trout, and over 400 river trout. I have sometimes thought of writing a book on trout and salmon fishing, in which my experience has been considerable, as I have fished more or less every season for five and sixty years; but so many books on the subject have of late years appeared, I am afraid that anything I could say would add but little to what the readers of those books already know.

Of the first twenty years of my fishing I have no record, as I did not keep one till 1848. Since that year the following is a list of the salmon, trout, and pike, I have killed:—

Salmon and peel (or grilse)	1,295
Sea trout	2,636
River and lake trout	65,436
Pike	602

The list would be much larger had I been able to include the earlier years, or had I been able to fish as often as I pleased; but my life has been a busy one, and, until I went to the Board of Works in 1863, I took no regular holidays, and could only spare a few days occasionally from my work. Since then, however, I have had a six weeks' holiday every year, which has been nearly always devoted to fishing. Of the trout in the above list, the great majority were the small ones of mountain streams, of which I have caught as many as seventeen dozen in a day; but in the rivers flowing through the rich lands in the midland and southern counties, I have killed many a fine basket of trout up to four pounds in weight, and in lakes up to eight pounds.

In my youth I fished a good deal in the Shannon, at Castleconnell, but have no account of my fishing there, though I had many a good day. My two boatmen were Mick Considine and Tom Enright, the former known as the "Little Boy," and afterwards as "The Badger;" the other as "Tom Pots." Every boatman on that part of the Shannon had a nickname. Poor old Tom Pots is now a blind ferryman at Castleconnell. I had not seen him for many years, but when crossing in his boat a few years ago, he recognized my voice. The change in Mick Considine's name occurred in this way. A Mr. Vincent and I were fishing near O'Brien's Bridge, and went into a farmhouse to have our dinner; a splendid salmon just caught, new potatoes, which the farmer dug for us, and newly churned butter made a meal not to be despised. After dinner Considine was standing near me; scarcely any men in those days wore beards, but he had a large one, and bushy whiskers too. "Mick," said I, "'Little Boy' is no name for you; you are like a badger, not like a boy." Then giving him a tap on the head with the handle of the gaff, "'The Badger'

I christen you, and 'The Badger' you are from this day forth." "Begorra, Mick," said Mrs. Frewen, the farmer's wife, "you are a badger in earnest now, for sure it's Mr. Le Fanu that can christen you; isn't he a dean's son?" From that day till his death, some years ago, he went by no other name.

It was at Castleconnell that I, with the help of these two boatmen, played a trick on the well-known S. C. Hall, which did him no harm beyond the loss of a hook, but gave him a fishing adventure to talk of for the rest of his life. I have since heard that a similar trick has been played on others, but to me and my boatmen it was original. Hall and Mrs. Hall were staying with us, late in the summer, at Castleconnell. Hall was, in a mild way, a devoted disciple of old Izaak, but up to this time he had never killed, or even hooked, a salmon; his fishing having been almost entirely confined to catching barbel, dace, and gudgeon, and other base fishes of the same sort, from a punt on the Thames. I once, and once only, had the privilege of enjoying that sport, it was near Teddington Lock; amongst other fish, I caught a gudgeon six inches long, or more; I think it must have been one of unusual size, as the boatman, who had disregarded the other fish, looked on it with evident admiration, laid it on his hand, apparently appraising its weight, and said, "That, sir, is an out-and-out gudgeon, and a gudgeon is the best fish as swims." But I must not digress.

Hall's ambition was to catch a salmon, and this it

is not easy to do when the water is low in bright, hot, autumn weather; the Shannon boatmen say, "The fish renaige the fly in August." I was, however, determined that, if I could not make him kill a fish, I would, at all events, give him some sport; so into the cot we got to troll, or as they call it there "to drag," the "Gariffs," a broad pool, too broad for throwing. On my line was a fly, on his a spinning bait, which I had basely leaded so heavily that it must before long sink to the bottom and stick. We had not been long out when it got fast in a sunken rock. The boatmen pulled hard away from the rock. Whirr! whirr! went the reel, as I shouted—

"You're in him, Hall! Raise your rod; don't let him get slack line."

"Begorra, he *is* in him, sure enough," said the Badger; "a big fish he is, too."

When about fifty yards of line were run out, back they rowed towards the rock, while we shouted to Hall, "Wheel on him! wheel quick on him or he'll go." As soon as his line was reeled up, and his rod well bent, off we went again—whirr! whirr! whirr! goes the reel, faster and louder than before. Hall was so excited, and so fully occupied, that he never saw nor suspected the manœuvres of the men. In this style we made him play the rock for over twenty minutes, when we finally rowed right away, till all his eighty yards of line were run out, except a few rolls on the axle of the wheel.

"What shall I do? what shall I do?" he cried. "He'll take all my line away!"

"You must hold on to him hard," I said, "and take your chance."

In another moment the casting-line snapped, the line slackened, the rod straightened.

"He's gone," cried Hall, throwing himself down in the bottom of the cot.

"Och, murdher! murdher!" shouted Tom Pots, "the milt is broke in me. What made your honour hould him so hard? Och, but he was a terrible big fish! that fish was fifty pounds if he was an ounce."

Hall, as many of my readers probably know, lived to a great age; but never to the day of his death did he cease to mourn the loss of that fish. How often, years after, have I, and other friends of his, heard him describe the play that fish gave, and what a monster he must have been!

Of late years, except an occasional day on other rivers, my salmon fishing has been confined to the Kerry Blackwater, and to the Mulcaire, in the county of Limerick. In the former I have killed sixteen salmon and peel in a day, and in the latter thirteen. In my earlier days I used a great variety of flies for trout. I have tied and tried nearly all the four dozen different kinds, which are so well described in "Ronald's Fly-fisher's Entomology," where there is given an exact coloured likeness of each fly, and of its artificial imitation.

Age and experience has taught me the folly of all this, as of many other things which I once thought wondrous wise. I am now reduced to a few simple patterns, though not quite to Cholmondely Pennell's three.

Of salmon flies I had at one time no end of different sorts, and loved to get a new pattern from some new book; I have seldom used any but those of my own tying, and for years have very rarely tied any but the four following:—

1. Tag yellow; body claret or fiery brown fur, with hackle of the same colour, ribbed with gold; yellow or jay hackle round shoulder.

2. Tag orange; body black silk and black hackle, ribbed with silver; jay hackle round the shoulder.

3. Tag yellow; body grey fur and grey hackle, ribbed with silver; yellow hackle round shoulder.

4. Grouse Lochaber; body orange or black, ribbed with gold.

The tail of each, a golden pheasant crest, with a few sprigs of summer duck. The wings nearly the same for all, of mixed fibres of golden pheasant's frills, tail, and red spears, green parrot, blue and yellow macaw, guinea-hen, mallard, and summer duck, or some of these; head, black ostrich. I do not mean to say that flies of other patterns may not kill as well, but these are my favourites everywhere. Of course I tie them of various sizes; and if one of them of the proper size will not raise and kill a fish, I fear it is the fault of the fisherman, not of the fly.

Though my faith in colour has not increased with time, my faith in size has. If I raise two or three fish without hooking one, or if a fish rise twice or thrice without taking, I put up a smaller fly of the same pattern, and generally do so with success. Many men, in my opinion, fish with flies too large, especially in low water.

In the Kerry Blackwater, a rapid mountain river, which may be in high flood in the morning and quite low in the evening, I often during the day use flies of five or six different sizes, reducing the size as the water falls; but in the Mulcaire, which continues for a day or two, or longer, without any perceptible change in the height or colour of the water, I seldom change the fly, which, as a rule, is no bigger than a white trout fly.

Spinning and worm-fishing for salmon are so well described in the Badminton Library and other books that I can add nothing, except that men are apt to strike too soon. In fly-fishing, too, I am inclined to think that, except in lakes or very still water, the rod should not be raised until a pull is felt. It is many a year since one of the best salmon-fishers I have known, when he saw me raise my rod on seeing a rise, said to me, "You should not do that; never pull a fish till he pulls you." In some parts of rivers you can see the fish come quietly at the fly, and how often have I seen an excited fisher pull the fly away from him before he had time to take it. I remember once, in my younger days, on my doing this my gillie said to me, "Did you see how sorrowful the salmon looked when your honour pulled the fly out of his mouth?"

Some people still find it hard to believe that the little smolts, which have lived for a year or more in the river, and have only grown six inches long, will return from the sea, after a visit of but two or three months, as grilse from four to seven pounds' weight, or even more. What food they thrive on so wonderfully in the sea has not, I think, been discovered. Dr. Edward Hamilton, indeed, in his "Recollections of Fly-fishing," a most interesting book, says, "They live chiefly upon small fish and crustacea; young herrings they delight in;" but, unfortunately, he does not give his authority for this statement. Whatever they feed on, the fact of their rapid growth is beyond dispute. It is the same with trout. Little trout, which have lived for years in a mountain stream, and have not grown to more than six or seven inches long, if transferred to a river flowing through rich lands, or to a newly made lake or pond, will increase in size nearly as rapidly as the smolts do on their transfer to the sea. This fact is well established; but the size they will attain in a few months is not so generally known.

My brother-in-law, Sir Croker Barrington, made a large pond, almost a little lake, of about twenty acres in extent, in his demesne at Glenstal, in the county of Limerick. The lake is fed by an overflowing spring well, and by a very small stream, in which there are no fish, as it dries up altogether in summer time. I saw the dam completed on the 1st of November, 1880; the lake then began to fill. My nephews, after that, caught in the neighbouring mountain streams a number of little trout, the largest not more than half a pound weight, and put them into the lake. I was there in the following July, and it was full of splendid fish, many three pounds and upwards. One of four and a half pounds was caught, and some larger ones were seen.

Amongst the fish put into the lake were many parr, or young salmon, five or six inches long. A fine wire grating was fixed at the exit from the lake to prevent their escape. By July they were about one and a half pound weight each, bright as silver, and very wild and plucky when hooked; excellent at table, too, the flesh pink and curdy. What became of them I do not know; they disappeared from the lake. The wire grating may have been broken or disturbed, and so they may have got away to the sea.

Though it is not known on what food salmon fatten in the sea, I have little doubt that what makes trout grow so fast in newly formed lakes and ponds is the great quantity of insect food they get from the submerged grasses and weeds. In rivers where the trout are large there is much insect food. If you pull up a bullrush or a reed you will find the part that was under water often quite covered with larva of flies and other insects; whereas in mountain

s

streams insect life is comparatively scarce. I have seen somewhere an account of experiments tried on trout by feeding one set exclusively on worms and small fish, and another set on flies and other insects. The latter grew and throve immensely better than the former.

It is strange that there is nothing found in the stomachs of salmon caught in rivers. I have often tried, but never could find anything. Many explanations have been offered, all, to my mind, quite unsatisfactory. In some rivers in time of flood you will catch salmon with a worm, or a bunch of two or three worms, and while the trout you then catch are full of worms, there is nothing in the salmon. One of my sons thinks the salmon may only chew and suck the worms, and then throw them out of their mouths. I can hardly believe this, but it is as likely as any other of the theories I have read of.

A remarkable property of trout and some other fish is the way in which their colour adapts itself to that of the bottom of the river on which they lie. It is this which makes it so hard to see them. This property is well known; but it is not, I think, so well known how quickly the colour changes. I have often tried a black vessel and a white one—putting three or four trout into each. In about two minutes or less those in the black vessel are so dark that you can scarcely see them, while those in the white vessel, in an equally short time, become a very pale brown or fawn-colour. If one of them is put in amongst the dark ones he looks almost white; but in a minute or two is as dark as the others, and *vice versâ* a black one amongst the bright ones. I have just got a dozen tin vessels made, painted of different colours, green, red, blue, etc., and I mean to try how far trout will take the different shades. Their colour certainly does adapt itself more or less to the green weeds, the blue limestone, or the brown sandstone of the river bottom, and no doubt many a fisher has observed, what I have often seen, that a trout lying on a gravelly bottom, composed of light and dark pebbles, has his body striped, each part assuming the colour of the pebble on which it lies.

Another strange fact is that in rivers where the trout are very small, you will occasionally find a huge fellow, a Brobdignag amongst the Lilliputians. I have had several examples of this. One was in the Dargle river, in which the trout are nearly all under a quarter-pound—a half-pounder is quite a rarity. I was fishing in the lower part of it one evening, and had hooked a little trout on my dropper-fly, but found that the tail-fly was held fast. I thought it had stuck in a stump or weed, until whatever it was began to move slowly across the river, with a very heavy weight upon the line. I was just thinking whether it might possibly be an otter, when out of the water sprang such a trout as I never dreamt could be there. My tackle was very light, and I was without a landing-net. However, after a long and exciting fight, I tired him, and drew him gently to the edge of a low strand, and as he lay there on his side, gave him a shove with my foot that sent him high and dry on *terra firma*. He was a little over five pounds, and by no means a badly shaped fish. As I went a little lower down, a stranger who had been fishing further up the stream, but had given it up, was looking into the river over the road wall. He asked me whether I had had any sport.

"Pretty good," said I. "I have got a few nice ones."

"I hear," said he, "they are very small in this river."

"They are rather small; you don't get many bigger than this one," said I, taking my monster out of the basket and holding him up.

The stranger gave utterance to a profane exclamation of surprise, and departed.

Higher up this river, just below Powerscourt demesne, is Tinahinch, the house and property which was given to Grattan by the Irish nation, in remembrance of his services to his country. The place was too much wooded, and has been much improved by Grattan's granddaughter, the present proprietor, who has cut down many of the old trees, which were far too numerous. Grattan was so fond of them that he would never allow one of them to be cut. An English friend, who had been staying with him, asked him whether he would be annoyed if he ventured to make a suggestion. "On the contrary," said Grattan, "I shall feel greatly obliged. "Well," said his friend, "don't you think that great beech tree is a little too close upon the house—rather overshadows it?" "I do," said Grattan; "and I have often thought of taking down the house."

The peasantry in most parts of Ireland admire no woman that is not fat and plump. The highest compliment they can pay is to tell a lady that she is growing fat. At our fishing quarters in Kerry we had a good example of this. On our arrival an old woman, Mary Sugrue by name, said to my wife, "Ah then, ma'am, you're looking grand entirely, God bless you! and you're fallen greatly into meat since you were here last year."

Another time, at Glenstal, my wife went to see the wife of the gamekeeper, a Mrs. Neal, who is very fat—at least three or four stone heavier than my wife. "Ah then, ma'am," said she, "I'm proud to see you looking so well and so fat." "Well," said my wife, "I don't think you have much to complain of in that respect, Mrs. Neal." "Ah ma'am," said she, "how could a poor woman like me be as fat as a lady like you?"

Small or thin men are not admired either. I heard of a sturdy beggar who said to a pale, emaciated youth who would not give him anything, "Bad luck to you, you desarter from the churchyard!"

Mrs. Martin of Ross told me that some short time ago, as she was going out for a walk, a poor woman was at the hall door, with whom she had the following conversation:—

Poor Woman. "Ah then, ma'am, God bless you! and won't you give your poor widdy something?"

Mrs. Martin. "But you are not a widow."

Poor Woman. "Begorra, I am, ma'am, and a very poor widdy, with three small childher."

Mrs. Martin. "But, my good woman, I know your husband perfectly well."

Poor Woman. "Of course you do, ma'am; but sure that poor little unsignificant craythur is not worth mentioning."

But to return to fishing. Twice in my life I have hooked two salmon together; each time I lost one and killed the other. I have, however, several times killed a salmon and a sea-trout together.

In fly-fishing I never caught a bird but once; it was a water ouzel. I also caught four bats; but they and the bird flew by chance against my line, and were hooked by the wing. I wonder a swallow never takes a fly. I saw a robin caught once. A friend of mine, when going in to luncheon, stuck his rod in the ground in front of the house, and on coming out found that a robin had taken one of the flies, a small black midge.

Like most fishers, I have hooked a good many men, myself most frequently. I never hooked a woman but once—it was my wife. I'm not making a miserable joke. I was fishing at Ballinahinch, in Connemara; she was sitting on a rock behind me, and I sent a salmon fly right into her chin as far as it could go. I don't know anything more disagreeable both to hooked and hooker; and I hate pulling the hook out, but I always do so instead of cutting it out or stripping off the fly and driving the hook through, and so drawing it out at another place. Losing your first salmon of the season just as he is into the gaff is bad enough, and getting the water well above your wading boots on a cold, frosty morning is not pleasant; but these accidents that a fisherman is heir to are mere nothings compared with what you feel when you find your salmon fly firmly embedded in your own or in some one else's face.

Another time, at Killarney, my attendant, Callaghan McCarthy, was behind me; I had made a cast, and heard him say, "Hold on, sir!" but, on the contrary, I gave a good chuck, thinking I had only stuck my fly in a weed or leaf behind me. He called out, "For God's sake, hold on, sir! Begorra, I believe it's what you want to pull the eye out of me." Sure enough my hook was right through his upper eyelid.

It was with this Callaghan McCarthy that I was once speaking of one of my assistants on the railway at Killarney, named Handcock, who was a very hot-tempered fellow, and rather severe with the men. "Well," said Callaghan to me, "they may say what they plase, your honour, about Mr. Handcock, but he's a wondherful feelin' gintleman." "I'm glad to hear you say so, Callaghan," said I. "Oh then, indeed, it's him that *is* the feelin' gintleman. When I was so bad last winther, didn't he come into the house to see me? And as soon as he seen me, 'McCarthy,' says he, 'put out your tongue.' Well, savin' yer honour's presence, I put out my tongue; and when he seen it, 'McCarthy,' says he, 'you're a dead man.' He's a rale feelin' gintleman, that's what he is."

At Glenstal I was going down, one warm evening, to fish the ponds. I had wound a cast of flies round my hat, and another round that of the under keeper. As we went down through the wood a great many flies were buzzing about us. I mistook one of those on my hat for one of them, made a slap at it, and sent the hook right into the palm of my hand. I could see that the keeper was with difficulty suppressing a laugh; but about ten minutes afterwards he called out, "Bedad, sir, I've done it myself now." And so he had, and in exactly the same way.

A Mr. Edward Dartnell told me that as he was fishing near Limerick for pike, with a frog for his bait, he in some way managed to send the hook right through the gristly part of his nose, between the nostrils. He had to walk a mile, the frog hanging there, but concealed beneath his pocket-handkerchief, till he came to a forge, and got the hook filed across and taken out.

On a cloudless day I was fishing on the river Laune at Killarney. It was so calm, and the water so clear, that I couldn't raise a fish, so I tried worms, and soon hooked a small salmon. While playing him I thought I saw something constantly darting at his head, and as he got tired and came near, I saw that it was a large perch, which was grabbing at the worms hanging on my hook from the salmon's mouth. He never ceased to do so till the fish was gaffed; and so bold was he, that if my gillie had had a large landing-net instead of a gaff, I am sure he would have landed both the fish.

One day, as I was fishing the Swords river, I got into conversation with McClelland, the water bailiff. He asked me how many children I had. I told him, and he said, "That's quare now, your honour, for that's exactly the same number myself and my missus has. And isn't it strange how the Lord would give you and me, that can't afford it, such a lot? and look at Mr. Roe, and Mr. Dargan, and other rich men that hasn't one. But I suppose," he continued after a pause—" I suppose the Lord takes some other way of tormenting them."

When fishing in Connemara, in the summer of 1869, I started one morning very early from Glendalough Hotel, our head-quarters, for the Snave Beg ("The Little Swim"), so called because it is the narrowest part of Ballinahinch Lake, in fact little more than a strait joining the upper to the lower lake. My wife and two children were, after their breakfast, to meet me there. By half-past nine I had killed two salmon, and in order to cast my fly over a fish that was rising a long way out, I stepped out from stone to stone on some slippery rocks. Just as I reached the point I was making for my feet went from under me, and I fell flat on my back into the lake. All my clothes, I need not say, required drying, so, as the sun was hot, I spread them on the rocks, and ran about across the heather to warm and dry myself. While I was still in this unusual fishing costume I heard the sound of a car rapidly approaching, and saw, to my horror, that not only were my wife and children upon it, but also another lady. Fortunately there was a large rock close by; behind this I carefully concealed myself, and despatched one of my boatmen to stop the car, and to ask them to send me a rug and as many pins as they could muster. The rug was pinned round me, my arms left free, and my legs sufficiently so to allow me to walk, and thus attired I fished for three full hours, until my clothes were dry.

I have had many other duckings, both in lake and river, besides the "Snave Beg" just described, but I shall only mention one of them, as they are usual incidents in the life of every fisherman. At our fishing quarters on the Kerry Blackwater most of the fishing is on the opposite side of the river from the house. We pull ourselves across in a flat-bottomed boat attached to an endless rope, which passes through pulleys on each bank. One wet and stormy day during our stay there, in the year 1884, I was watching for a fresh in the river, and from the house I could see that the water was slowly rising; so I sallied forth with rod and gaff and my trusty attendant, Andy Hallissy. We got into the boat, and he began to pull us across, while I remained standing up, with the rod in one hand and the gaff in the other. We had got about halfway, when a sudden gust of wind drove us against the rope, which caught me across the chest, and sent me spinning over the gunwale of the boat into the water. I at once struck out to swim ashore, but found that I made no progress, the reason, which I soon discovered, being that Andy had firm hold of the tails of my coat. "Let go, Andy," I said, "and I'll be ashore in a minute." "Begorra, I won't let you go," said Andy, "until you catch hold of the gunwale of the boat; and I'll pull you over myself." Within an hour I had been up to the house, had changed my clothes, and was playing a salmon.

At Killarney I heard the following story, which shows how differently an Irishman and a Scotchman will take a joke. An Englishman, who had been fishing the lower lake, said to his boatman, "An extraordinary thing happened to me some years ago. I lost a pair of scissors out of my fishing book at the edge of the lake. The next year I was fishing here again and hooked and killed a very large pike. I felt something hard inside him, so I opened him, and what do you think it was?" "Begorra, then, your honour, I'd think it moight be your scissors only for one little thing." "What is that?" asked the other. "It's only just this, your honour, that there never was a pike in any of the Killarney lakes since the world began."

Afterwards he tried the same story with a gillie in Scotland. When he asked him, "What do you think was inside him?" the gillie replied, "Your scissors and nae guts; and the Duke of Argyll—and he's a far greater man than the king—would not have insulted me sae. I'll fish nae mare wi ye;" and off he walked.

At Lareen, the fishing quarters of my brother-in-law, the late Chief Justice May, I was fishing down the Bundrowse river, accompanied by his keeper Watt. I was crossing to an island by some stepping stones, when he called out to me not to go that way as the stones were slippery; "and," said he, "you might fall in as his lordship did the other day; but I have made a nice little bridge at the other end of the island, and he never crosses by the stones now."

"I suppose," said I, "he dreads the water as a burnt child dreads the fire."

"That's just it," said Watt. "But maybe you don't know who it was that invented that saying."

"I do not know," I said. "I don't think it was Solomon."

"No, it wasn't him," said he; "it was my grandfather."

"Indeed," said I. "I thought it was more ancient."

"Well, it isn't, though it's wonderful how well known it is; but it was my grandfather that first said it. You see, sir, this was the way it came about. My grandfather was a smith, and he saw the minister coming down towards the forge to pay him a visit, and for a bit of a joke he threw a small bit of iron he was forging on the ground; it was nearly red hot. When the minister came in, after a little talk, my grandfather says to him, 'Minister, might I trouble you to hand me up that bit of iron there at your feet?' So minister picked it up; but I can tell you he dropped it quick enough, for it burnt his fingers. Just that minute my father and my uncle came into the forge—they were wee chaps then—and my grandfather he says to them, 'Boys, hand me up that bit of iron.' Well, the little fellows they knelt down and just spit on the iron to see was it too hot; so my grandfather he began to laugh at the minister, and says to him, 'Well now, minister, with all your book-reading and learning you see you haven't the wit of them two small chaps.' 'Ah!' says minister, 'I suppose you played them that trick before, and they didn't want to burn their fingers again.' 'That's just it, minister,' says my grandfather. 'You see, a burnt child dreads the fire.' So the minister told the story everywhere, and that's the way the saying got spread all over the country. So, you see, my grandfather invented it."

This Watt had been keeper to Lord Massey,

from whom my brother-in-law rented the place, and the fishing and shooting; and I think it was with him that Lord Spencer many years before had rather an amusing adventure. In May, 1870, during his first viceroyalty, Lord Spencer asked me to accompany him and Lady Spencer part of the way on a tour they were about to make through the north and north-west of Ireland. After having visited Lough Erne, Enniskillen, and Belleek, we arrived at Bundoran late in the evening, and here I was to have left them. Lord Spencer, however, pressed me to remain with them the next day in order to go with him to fish the Bundrowse river, which he said Lord Massey had invited him to try if he should ever be in the neighbourhood. I should have greatly liked to do so, as I had never seen the Bundrowse, and had heard much of it, not only as a salmon river, but as famous for the curious and beautiful gillaroo trout, which abound in it and in Lough Melvin, from which it flows to the sea. Unfortunately, however, engagements in Dublin necessitated my departure, and I left them next morning before they started for Lareen, which lies about four miles to the south of Bundoran.

I did not see Lord Spencer till about ten days afterwards, when I was dining at the Viceregal Lodge. I then asked him whether he had had good sport the day I left him.

"Didn't you hear what happened?" he said. "We had a funny adventure, but no fishing. We arrived," he went on, "at the river and had just put up our rods, when a keeper appeared and inquired whether we had an order from Lord Massey. Freddy Campbell — he was then Lord Spencer's aide-de-camp—explained to him who we were, and that Lord Massey had asked me to fish. The keeper replied, 'If you haven't a written order I won't let you fish, not even if you were the king, let alone the lord lieutenant.' Persuasion was useless; the keeper was inexorable, and we had to take down our rods and return sadly to Bundoran."

"Oh, sir," I said, "Lord Massey will be greatly annoyed and very angry about it."

"No," he said; "I took care about that. I wrote to him the same day to tell him that I was delighted to have found such an honest and trustworthy keeper."

CHAPTER XVIII.

Illicit stills—Getting a reward—Poteen—Past and present—Dress and dwellings—Marriage and language—Material improvement since 1850.

SOME twenty years ago one of my sons, then a boy, and I were on a fishing excursion in the county of Donegal. We were staying at the little village of Glen, close by Glen Lough, in rooms over a public-house, kept by one Dolty McGarvey. After a few days he had become a great friend of ours. I knew a great deal of poteen (illicit whisky) was distilled there, and as I had, in all my rambles, never seen an illicit still, I greatly wished to see one. I imparted my wish to Dolty, and he at once said he would take us to see one the next day; so early on the morrow he brought us some miles across wild hills and bogs till we arrived at the house of a farmer, who was his partner in the still. They brought us on some way till we came to a lane, well sheltered by thorn bushes, where, by a little stream, three sons of Dolty's partner, fine young fellows as I ever saw, were working at the still. They wore stockings, but no shoes, and told us that by that means, in case of alarm, they could run more quickly over rocks and rough ground than if they were barefoot or had shoes. We sat on a bank, and they drank our health and we drank theirs, in a little measure, not much bigger than a thimble, of the poteen hot from the still. I asked Dolty whether the smoke ever attracted the attention of the police. He said that the distilling itself made so little smoke that it was unnoticed at a short distance, but that drying the malt made a great deal, and it was then they had to be careful.

"How do you manage to escape, then?" I asked.

"Ah!" said he, "we always dry the malt in the beginning of July, when all the police are taken off to Derry to put down the riots there; so we can do it safely then. God is good, sir; God is good."

A few mornings after this he roused us up very early, and told us to look out of our window, from which we saw five policemen carrying in triumph through the village a still, which they had just seized. Dolty was in fits of laughter. On our asking what he laughed at, he told us that the still was an old one, quite worn out.

"Look at the holes in it," he said. "Some one has given information to the police where they would find it. We often play them that trick, and sometimes get a pound reward for an old still that isn't worth sixpence."

On our return to Dublin I told my friend T——
of our adventures. An Englishman he was, on the
Lord Lieutenant's (Lord Spencer's) staff; he had
been studying Irish characters and habits, and was
most anxious to see an illicit still at work, so off he
set to Glen, and put up at Dolty McGarvey's. The
morning after his arrival—it was rather premature
—he said to him—

"Can you take me to see a still at work? I
should like to see one."

"There is no still in the country," said Dolty.

"Nonsense," said T——. "You took Mr. Le
Fanu to see one."

"Who told you that, sir?" said Dolty. "I
couldn't show him one, for there is not one
here."

"'Twas Mr. Le Fanu himself who told me," said
T——.

"He was humbugging you," said McGarvey.
"He never saw a still here."

Before I again visited that part of Donegal
Dolty McGarvey had died, so I never heard why he
wouldn't do by my friend as he had done by us.
Perhaps he had seen the royal arms on T——'s
despatch-box, or on the seals on letters from the
Castle, and feared he might be a detective or a spy;
but whatever it was, my friend's wish to see a still
at work has never been gratified.

It is a curious fact that in parts of Donegal they
grow a crop of oats and barley mixed; they call it

pracas (which is the Irish for a mixture), and use it for no other purpose but illicit distilling.

Since the time of my visit to the still with Dolty McGarvey, illicit distilling in that part of Donegal has, I believe, much diminished, owing to a great extent to the exertions of the late Lord Leitrim, whose early death has been such a loss not only to his own tenantry, whose welfare he always had at heart, and by whom he was much beloved, but to the whole of the countryside, which he had benefited in many ways, especially by the establishment of steamers plying between Mulroy Bay and Glasgow. But though illicit distilling has to a great extent died out on the mainland, it has been found impossible to suppress it on the islands off the west coast. Constabulary had for some time been stationed on several of the largest of these islands, but they were in some cases withdrawn about eighteen months ago. Whatever the reasons for this step may have been, the results cannot but be disastrous to the inhabitants of the islands and the adjoining parts of the mainland, to which the poteen is easily smuggled. It is only a few days ago that I received a letter from a friend of mine who had just visited one of the islands off the coast of Sligo. The following is an extract from his letter:—

"We made an expedition to Inishmurray the day before yesterday. . . . We saw the old churches and the beehive cells, and the image of Father Molash. The island was once an island of the saints; it is now one of devils. Most of the men were more or less drunk; the air seemed laden with fumes of poteen. We saw a couple of stills, one at work. The schoolmaster says that the children are getting quite dull and stupid from being constantly given tastes of the whisky."

The manufacture is an ancient one. No doubt the "Aqua Vitæ," which Holinshed in his "Chronicles" mentions as an "ordinarie drinke" of the inhabitants, was nothing but the poteen of the olden times. I cannot do better than to give a quotation of the passage in the "Chronicles," in which its wonderful virtues are so well described.

"The soile is low and waterish, including diverse little Islands, invironed with lakes and marrish. Highest hils have standing pooles in their tops. Inhabitants, especiallie new come, are subject to distillations, rheumes and fluxes. For remedie whereof they use an ordinarie drink of Aquæ Vitæ, being so qualified in the making, that it drieth more and also inflameth lesse than other hot confections doo. One Theoricus wrote a proper treatise of Aquæ Vitæ wherein he praiseth it to the ninth degree. He distinguisheth three sorts thereof, Simplex, Composita, and Perfectisima. He declareth the simples and ingrediences thereto belonging. He wisheth it to be taken as well before meat as after. It drieth up the breaking out of hands, and killeth the flesh worms, if you wash your hands therewith. It scowreth all scurfe and scalds from the head, being therewith dailie washt before meales. Being moderatlie taken (saith he) it sloweth age, it strengthneth youth, it helpeth digestion, it cutteth flegme, it abandoneth melancholie, it relisheth the heart, it lighteneth the mind, it quickeneth the spirits, it cureth the hydropsie, it healeth the strangurie, it keepeth and preserveth the head from whirling, the eies from dazeling, the toong from lisping, the mouth from maffling, the teeth from chattering, and the throte from ratling: it keepeth the weasan from stifling, the stomach from wambling, and the heart from swelling, the hands from shivering, the sinewes from shrinking, the veines from crumpling, the bones from aking, the marrow from soaking. Ulstadius also ascribeth thereto a singular praise, and would have it to burne being kindled, which he taketh to be a token to know the goodnesse thereof. And trulie it is a sovereigne liquor if it be orderlie taken."

It is hard to realize how great the change in nearly everything has been since my early days.

I was a child when steam vessels first plied between England and Ireland; before that passengers and mails, as well as goods, were carried across the channel by sailing vessels.

The mail-boats started from the Pigeon-house, near Dublin. In bad weather the voyage often occupied some days, and in view of a not improbable long sea voyage, each passenger took with him a hamper of provisions, which, if the passage proved a good one, was given to the captain as a perquisite. A ferry-boat carried passengers and mails across the Menai Straits.

I remember well the opening of the first railway in England. I had entered college before one existed here. The earliest was that from Dublin to Kingstown, on which I travelled in the first train that ever ran in Ireland.

I can recollect the time, before gas was used as an illuminant, when towns and cities were lighted by oil lamps. It was in those days that an old lady, on being told that oil would be altogether superseded by gas, asked with a sigh, "And what will the poor whales do?"

There were no matches in my early days; the want was supplied by flint and steel, or tinder-box.

I need hardly say there were no telegraphs nor telephones nor photographs. The world, indeed, has "wagged a pace."

In the dress and habits of the country people, too, there has been much change. The dress of girls and women on Sundays and holidays is now as close an imitation as they can afford or procure of that of fashionable ladies. Formerly, instead of shawls or capes, they wore over a simple gown a long cloak with a hood. In many parts of the south it was of bright scarlet cloth, the hood lined with pink silk. Hats and bonnets were unknown. Girls had nothing on their heads; married women wore many-bordered, high-cauled caps. The men all wore corduroy knee-breeches, bright coloured waistcoats, and frieze coats, made like an evening coat.

The red cloaks and white caps, contrasting with the grey and blue frieze, gave a wonderfully picturesque effect to a funeral or other procession, where all walked, except some farmers, who rode with their wives on pillions behind them. This effect in funerals was heightened by the wild, wailing Irish cry, "keened" by many women all the way from the home to the grave. Now it is only heard in the churchyard, and rarely even there.

In the food of the people, too, there has been great improvement. In old days most of them had nothing but potatoes; now there are very few who have not, in addition, bread and tea, and not unfrequently meat of some kind.

Their dwellings also are much improved. Formerly the number of cabins with but one room or two, a kitchen and a bedroom, was very large. In them there were two beds, in one of which slept the father and mother of the family; in the other, the children, who lay (as they called it) " heads and points," the heads of the boys being at one end of the bed, those of the girls at the other. These houses were built of mud. Most of them had no windows; only a hole in the wall to let out the smoke. Such dwellings are disappearing fast, and ere many years none of them will, I trust, be left. The houses built in recent years are comfortable and substantial.

Now, in every house, there are candles or a lamp. Formerly, as a rule, there were neither; the inmates sat and talked by the light of the turf fire, and, if anything had to be searched for, they lit a rush, which served in lieu of a candle. Of them there was a good supply. They were peeled rushes, dried, and drawn through melted grease or oil. The peasants who came to us for medicine always begged for castor-oil. We suspected they generally wanted it not for their own insides, but for the outsides of their rushes; all the more because we knew that they had a strong objection to take it as a medicine, believing, as many of them did, that it was made from human flesh boiled down. This is why an angry man would say to another—or, for that matter, to his wife if she annoyed him—" It's what I ought to put you into the pot on the fire and boil you into castor-oil."

The arrangements as to marriages have not changed as much as other things. It very often happened, and sometimes happens still, that the bride and bridegroom never saw each other till the wedding day, or a day or two before it; the match being made by the parents, assisted by the priest. Of course there were love matches too; but they were the exceptions.

Farmers had a great objection to their younger daughters being married before the elder ones. A tenant of my brother-in-law, Sir William Barrington, came to tell him that his daughter Margaret had been married the day before to Pat Ryan. " How is that?" said he; " he told me it was your daughter Mary he was going to marry." " So it was, your honour," said the farmer. " 'Twas her he was courting, but I made him take Margaret. Wasn't she my ouldest daughter? and I wouldn't let him be runnin' through the family that way, taking his pick and choice of them." Mary was young and pretty, Margaret *passée* and plain. It was probably in such a case that a man, boasting of the kindness of his father-in-law, said, " Sure he gave me his ouldest daughter, and if he had an oulder one he'd have given her to me."

The greater part of the income of the priests

was derived from weddings. There was always a collection for "his raverence." At the wedding of the daughter of a farmer, Tom Dundon, living near us at Abington, at which I was present, the priest got over thirty pounds. That was one of the cases in which the bride and bridegroom never met until their wedding day, and a very happy married life they had.

Not the least remarkable of the changes in recent years is the rapidity with which the Irish language is dying out, and in many districts has died out. This is mainly due to the education in the national schools, where all the teaching is in English, and to the want of books or newspapers in Irish.

In the counties of Limerick and Tipperary, when I was a boy, many of the old people could speak Irish only; middle-aged men and women knew both English and Irish, but always spoke the latter to each other; boys and girls understood both languages, but almost always spoke in English. Now it is only very old men and women who know Irish there; the young people do not understand it, and cannot tell the meaning of any Irish word. The same process is going on, though not everywhere so rapidly, in every district, where fifty years ago Irish was the language of the people; and I fear that, notwithstanding the endeavours of a society started not long ago to keep it alive, the Irish language will, before another fifty years, be dead.

CHAPTER XIX.

The science of hypnotism—Early experiments and lessons—A drink of cider—I convert Isaac Butt—All wrong—A dangerous power.

I HAVE hitherto dealt almost entirely with my recollections of Ireland and Irishmen, but it may not be uninteresting if I insert a brief account of my personal experiences in a science, if it may be so called, which is still full of difficulty and mystery. I have ventured to call it a science, as the study given to it in recent years in France and elsewhere has led to a greater sense of its importance than formerly existed. I refer to hypnotism, or electro-biology, as it was called when I first experimented in it, from its supposed connection with electricity, and with the relation of electricity to human life.

As many people may never have witnessed the extraordinary phenomena connected with it, or may have only seen them at public exhibitions, and consequently believed them to be merely the result of collusion between the exhibitor and some of his audience, I will give some instances of experiments

I myself made many years ago, though they have, no doubt, been frequently repeated since by others.

It was over forty years ago that my attention was first called to the subject. I happened, when in London in 1851, to attend a public exhibition given by a man named Stone, and submitted myself as one of the subjects for his experiments. I found he was able to affect me to some extent, though only as far as my muscular movements were concerned. He could not get further than preventing me from opening or shutting my eyes, or from speaking without stuttering; but a friend who accompanied me was completely under his control. I was so much interested—for I had gone believing that the exhibition was a farce—that I called on Stone a few days afterwards to see whether I could learn anything from him. He gave me a lesson in his method of proceeding, and supplied me with a number of small discs of zinc, about an inch in diameter, with a piece of copper inserted in the centre. One of these was placed in the hand of each subject, who was told to look at it and keep quiet for a short time. The supposition was that these discs had, from their composition, some electric effect. But I subsequently found that they were quite unnecessary, and that any other small object would do as well; in fact, in some cases, especially where the conversation had been for some time on the subject, no preliminary preparation at all was required.

I very soon afterwards began experimenting on my own account. My usual method was to place one of the discs I have mentioned, or any small object, in the hand of each of the persons to be experimented on, and to ask them to remain quiet for a few minutes—I did not find that more than five minutes was ever required—I then removed the discs and told each subject to close his eyes, and to keep them closed till I returned. As soon as I had removed the disc from the last of them, I returned to the first, and pressing my left hand on his head and holding his hand in my right, I said to him, " You can't open your eyes; I defy you to open your eyes." If he opened his eyes without difficulty or evident exertion, I knew at once he would not make a good subject, and went no further with him. I generally found, however, that out of a dozen persons, there were one or two who either could not open their eyes at all, or did so with much difficulty. They frequently said it was because I was pressing my left hand so hard on their foreheads. In such cases I at once repeated the experiment without putting my hand to their head, but still holding their hand with mine. They were never able to open their eyes, but often made one more struggle, saying that it was my holding their hand which prevented them. I then repeated the experiment a third time without touching them at all, and invariably with the same result.

I next went on to other experiments, first trying

those which only affected their muscular action, such as preventing them from opening their mouths, and making them jump or stand in one spot as long as I wished. When I wanted to permit the subjects to regain their freedom of will, I always said, "All right;" and it is a curious fact that if, when they were entirely under my influence, I even accidentally happened to say, "All right," they at once recovered. I frequently found that I could not get beyond these muscular effects, but over the best subjects I was able to obtain such complete mastery, that they at once saw, believed, and did anything I *suggested*. I purposely use this word, for I found that however good the subject, or complete my power over him, I could not make him do anything without actual verbal suggestion. I have repeatedly tried with the very best subjects to affect them by the power of my will alone, and never with the slightest success. How great this power of suggestion was, may be gathered from a few instances.

Amongst many good subjects, whom I had found soon after I began experimenting, was a youth, a nephew of Hackett, the well-known fishing-tackle manufacturer in Cork. I had been talking one day on the subject of electro-biology to Father O'Sullivan, whom I have already mentioned under his name of Father Rufus, and he told me he could not believe in the possibility of such phenomena. I asked him to come some day and see me experiment with this youth. A few days afterwards he met me at

Hackett's house, and in his presence I made the boy imagine he was a dog and bark; see a cherry tree growing out of the table, pluck the fruit off it, and offer it to us; and, in fact, do and see anything I suggested to him.

Father Rufus was still unconvinced, and evidently half thought that there might be collusion. He asked me to come into another room, and, taking a bottle from his pocket, said—

"If you make him drink this, and think it is delicious cider, I shall admit that there is something in it."

On being assured by him that the contents of the bottle were perfectly harmless, I emptied it into a glass, returned to the other room, and said to the lad—

"I'm going to give you the nicest cider you ever drank. Don't drink it off too quickly, for it is particularly nice."

He sipped it with the greatest delight till the glass was nearly empty, when I restored him to his ordinary senses by saying, "All right." His grimaces were wonderful to behold, and he was nearly sick. Father Rufus was absolutely convinced. He had been to a chemist and had asked him to prepare a mixture of the most disgusting and nauseous, but at the same time harmless, drugs, and this was the stuff which the unfortunate youth had sipped with such evident relish.

I have often given subjects a piece of common yellow soap, telling them it was a delicious cake.

They always showed signs of the greatest enjoyment as they bit off a piece and began to munch it. I took care before they had time to swallow any of it to undeceive them, and I need hardly say they never showed any desire to swallow it after the magic words "All right" were spoken, while their grimaces were quite as amusing as those of the youth in Cork when he drank his cider.

Another unbeliever whom I converted was Isaac Butt. He and two fellow barristers were at the assizes in Cork, and came out to spend the day with me at Rathpeacon. I had no subjects, whom I had before tried, at hand, so in the evening I got eight lads who had been at work on the railway, which I had been constructing there. After the usual preliminary trials, I found two who were perfectly susceptible to my influence. I made them go through many performances, and among other things I prevented them from picking up a shilling from the ground. Butt objected that I might easily have promised them half a crown not to pick up the shilling. I told him that he might apply any test he wished.

"Try them," he said, "with five pounds, and I'll believe it."

I put five sovereigns on the gravel drive where we were standing, and said to the lads, "Boys, you shall have those five sovereigns if you can take them up; but your fingers cannot go within an inch of them."

It was wonderful to see the struggle they made, and how they rooted up the gravel to within an inch of the little pile of money, but they could not touch it. To complete Butt's conversion, I placed the five sovereigns on the hand of one of the lads, and said to him—

"If you keep those on your hand for three minutes, you shall, on my word of honour, have them for yourself."

I told Butt to take the time by his watch, and then said to the boy, "They're burning your hand—they're burning a hole in your hand; if you keep them any longer, they will burn a hole *right through* your hand."

The lad began blowing on his hand and moving the coins, as if they were burning him, and, long before the time was up, flung them on the ground with a cry of pain. Butt all the time had been patting him on the back, and telling him to keep the coins, for it was all humbug; but the answer was—

"What a humbug it is! Can't you see my hand is destroyed? Look at the hole in it."

I have recently read of cases where a subject is said to have been affected by some one from a distance, but, in those cases at least in which the effect is produced by a telegram, it appears to me to be practically nothing more nor less than suggestion. I have myself sometimes made suggestion produce its effect, after I had left the subject. I remember one day as I was leaving my gate lodge to walk into Cork, I said to my gatekeeper's servant-girl, who had already shown herself a good subject, "When I pass Ben Deeble's Mill, your eyes will shut, and they will not open again till I come home from Cork in the evening." The mill was about a quarter of a mile down the road, and I knew that curiosity would make her watch me till I passed it. The moment I got by the mill, I ran back to the lodge, and here I found the gatekeeper and his wife endeavouring to open the girl's eyes, which were shut fast. Their efforts were all in vain. As soon as they raised the eyelid of one eye and turned their attention to the other, the one they had opened closed again; and I have no doubt, if I had not intervened, her eyes would have remained shut till the evening.

It would be tedious to multiply instances. There was absolutely nothing that I could not persuade a person once under control to do or see. I have made a lady, who had the greatest horror of rats, imagine that my pocket-handkerchief, which I held rolled up in my hand, was one, and when she rushed away terrified, I made her think she was a cat, and she at once began to mew, seized the pocket-handkerchief in her teeth, and shook it. I have made people believe they were hens, judges, legs of mutton, generals, frogs, and famous men; and this in rapid succession. Indeed, so complete was their obedience, that I have again and again refused, when asked, to suggest to them that they were dead.

I was really afraid of the result that might possibly ensue.

After a person had been once successfully experimented on, it was not necessary, except possibly after a long interval, to repeat any of the preliminaries. I have often met a subject days and even weeks after he had been first affected, and have found him at once under my control. I remember meeting a Mr. D—— in the street in Cork, and after exchanging a few words of ordinary conversation, I suddenly said to him, "Good-bye; you can't stir from that spot, till I come back;" and there he was fixed, in spite of all his entreaties, till I chose to let him go, which I did in a minute or two, when I saw passers-by attracted by his struggles to move on.

It might be supposed that such experiments might have made one unpopular with those affected; but I always found that so far from diminishing any friendly feelings that existed, they appeared to strengthen them.

Once, and once only, did I feel myself in a difficulty. I had made a cousin of mine unable to speak without stuttering. To my horror, the magic words "All right" failed to produce their usual effect, and, in spite of all my efforts, I could not restore the power of speaking properly; in fact, my cousin continued to stutter more or less for some weeks.

I gave up experimenting long ago, and from

all that I have since read and heard on the subject, I think it is not one which should be meddled with except by those who are really investigating it scientifically; for as I learnt, from the instance I have just mentioned, it is impossible to know what may occur; and although the effects are undoubtedly very amusing to watch, they may possibly be more injurious to the person affected than they appear to be; while the power is so great that in the hands of an unscrupulous person it might become very dangerous.

CHAPTER XX.

Catholic Emancipation, 1829—The tithe war of 1832—The great famine of 1846—The Fenian agitation of 1865—France against England—Land-hunger—Crime and combination—Last words.

As I have passed a long life, well over seventy years, almost altogether in Ireland, and have constantly come in contact with every class in the country, and as I may, I think, fairly claim to have a considerable knowledge of its people, I trust I shall be excused for making a few remarks, before I conclude this book, on the present state of affairs, as seen by one who has personally observed the many agitations and the many changes in the condition of the country, which have occurred since the early part of the century.

The first great agitation which I remember was that for Catholic Emancipation, which was granted in 1829 under the pressure of a fear of an Irish rebellion. The great meetings and marchings to which I have already referred, had led the Duke of Wellington, then Prime Minister, to fear that

Ireland was ripe for a rebellion, more serious than that of '98, the danger and bloodshed of which he was unwilling to face. I can well remember the exaggerated notions the peasantry had of all the benefits they were to derive from the measure. Wages were at once to be doubled, and constant, well-paid employment to be given to every man.

My father and mother had been always ardently in favour of Catholic Emancipation, and were delighted when the Act was passed. On the night when the news that the bill had become law reached our part of the country, we were all assembled to see the bonfires which blazed on all the mountains and hills around us, and I well remember the shouting and rejoicings on the road that passed our gate, and the hearty cheers given for us. I specially recollect one man, a farmer named James Fleming, generally known as Shamus Oge (Young James), being asked by some one in the crowd what emancipation meant. "It means," said he, "a shilling a day for every man as long as he lives, whatever he does." The ordinary wages of the labourers were then sixpence a day.

We little thought on that night how soon we should see the same fires lighted all around us, when any of the clergy near us had suffered outrage, or how soon, without any change on our part, we should be hooted and shouted at whenever we appeared.

It is now nearly forgotten that in 1825, four

years earlier, a bill for Catholic Emancipation was passed in the House of Commons, and at the same time a bill by virtue of which the Roman Catholic priests would have received payment from the State, and been made entirely independent of the voluntary contributions of their congregations. One of the main facts that has to be borne in mind by any one who desires to judge fairly of the influence exercised by the Roman Catholic priesthood over their people in any great crisis, is this, that they are so entirely dependent for their sole means of support on the goodwill of the people, that they must always to a greater extent than is desirable follow, instead of lead, those over whom they are placed. If this bill had passed into law, there can be little doubt that the whole influence of the Roman Catholic priesthood would have been thrown into the opposite scale from that in which it has been during the last fifty years, and that the whole course of events in Ireland would have been very different. The bills were, however, unfortunately thrown out by the House of Lords, and when emancipation was granted, it was not accompanied by the other measure which had in 1825 been joined to it.

After the passing of the Emancipation Act comparative quiet reigned in the country till 1832, when the tithe war, with all its outrages, began. This agitation was carried out by O'Connell, on nearly the same lines as that for emancipation, and was crowned with like success. But the abolition of tithes did not bring to the peasantry all the benefits they expected; it merely changed the tithe into a rent-charge payable to the landlords, who were made liable for the payment of the clergy.

The success which attended the agitations for Catholic Emancipation and for the abolition of tithes —which success was in large measure due to the fear the English people entertained of an Irish rebellion—led O'Connell to commence his agitation for the repeal of the Union. This, however, failed, and its failure resulted in O'Connell's fall.

Great meetings had been held all through the country, at which O'Connell and others had used language more threatening than had been ventured on in the former agitations. Encouraged by the non-interference of the Government, O'Connell announced that a monster meeting would be held at Clontarf, close to Dublin, on Sunday, the 8th of September, 1843.

The Government determined that the meeting should not take place; a proclamation was issued forbidding it, and it was arranged that all the leaders of the agitation should be arrested. The duty of arresting O'Connell himself was assigned to Colonel Brown, the Chief Commissioner of Police, whom I have already mentioned in connection with my only attempt to enlist in that force. The excitement was intense; but at the last moment O'Connell struck his colours, and issued a second proclamation forbidding the people to meet. I was at Clontarf on the day fixed for the meeting. Nearly the whole of the garrison of Dublin—horse, foot, and artillery—was there, but no meeting was held. The subsequent prosecution and imprisonment of O'Connell and the other principal leaders put a complete stop to the agitation; and although it is true that their conviction was shortly afterwards quashed, after an appeal to the House of Lords, O'Connell's power was gone for ever.

Before the next agitation of any moment, the great famine of 1846-7 occurred. Up to that time the number of the people, and their poverty, steadily increased, and the first change for the better in their condition, within my memory, was subsequent, and in a great measure due, to that terrible affliction. It put a stop in some degree to the subdivision of holdings, which had been carried on to such an extent that, in many parts of the country, the holdings were so small that even had they been rent free they would have been insufficient for the maintenance of their occupiers. It forced the people not to depend in future on the potatoes as their staple food, and it led to some extent to better cultivation of the soil. The famine had hardly ended when Smith O'Brien's abortive rebellion occurred. Although earnest and able men—such as O'Brien himself, Tom Davies, Meagher, Mitchell, and others—were the leaders in the movement, it was an almost ludicrous failure; the hearts of the people were not in it, and the Roman Catholic priesthood were opposed to it.

For seventeen years after this time no agitation worth recording arose, and, with the exception of some isolated outrages, peace prevailed in the country, and the prosperity of all classes increased. Then in 1865 the Fenian Society came into existence, and continued to increase in power and in the number of members enrolled, until in February, 1866, the Habeas Corpus Act was suspended. Immediately before this a large number of Americans or Irish-Americans, easily recognizable by their dress and appearance, were to be met walking about the streets of Dublin. These gentlemen must somehow have got a hint of what was about to happen, for, on the day before the suspension of the Act, their sudden disappearance from the city was as remarkable as their previous appearance there had been. This conspiracy was not completely put down till March, 1867, when the principal Fenian army succumbed at Tallaght, a few miles from Dublin, to twelve men of the Royal Irish Constabulary, and smaller risings in other parts of Ireland at the same time were easily suppressed.

What I have called the principal Fenian army was in reality only a mob of half-armed and utterly undisciplined Dublin youths, who had assembled near this village of Tallaght. When opposed by the small force of constabulary, who fired a few shots, they retired to a neighbouring hill. Many of them dispersed during the night, but a considerable number remained till the morning, when they surrendered to a military force, and were marched into Dublin. I did not myself see the prisoners, but I remember my brother telling me how he had seen them, so tired out that, wet as it was, they were lying about on the ground, in the Castle yard. My brother's pantry-boy had joined the army, but was one of those who escaped being made prisoner, and he used to give a most interesting account of the Battle of Tallaght.

The agitation for Home Rule, begun by Isaac Butt, never appeared to me to have any reality in it until Parnell became the leader of the movement.

Looking back on these various agitations to which I have briefly referred, it appears to me that none of those which appealed merely to the anti-English sentiment of the people, ever obtained any real hold of the peasantry. Those which did succeed appealed to feelings of an entirely different nature, and aimed at the abolition of some religious inequality or some pecuniary burden, and there are few who would now deny the justice of Catholic Emancipation and of the abolition of the tithe system in Ireland.

I do not mean to suggest, by what I have just written, that the anti-English feeling is not a real thing. It is, on the contrary, as far as my observation goes, a very deep and far-reaching sentiment; and I have had opportunities of forming an opinion, from conversations with many of the peasantry in different parts of the country, whom I have known from their early youth, and who have not been afraid, as they generally are, to tell the real feelings entertained by themselves and their neighbours.

Their chief hope has always appeared to lie in a successful rebellion, by the aid of America, or, possibly, of France. Many of them have looked forward all their lives to " the War," as they call it. It is not long since a tenant of my brother-in-law, when on his death-bed, said to him, " Ah, yer honour, isn't it too bad entirely that I'd be dying now, and the War that I always thought I'd live to see coming so near?" The strength of the feeling was shown by the wild burst of enthusiasm in favour of the French at the beginning of the Franco-Prussian War, when processions marched through Dublin and other towns in Ireland, with tricolor banners, and led by bands playing the " Marseillaise." This sympathy with the French was undoubtedly due to the tradition of the help that had been expected from France in 1798, and to the hope that, if necessary, help against England might again be obtained from the same quarter.

But, strong as this anti-English feeling is, it is

not in it, as I think, that the real strength of the
agitation of the last fifteen years has lain. If it had
been founded on this alone, or even mainly on this,
it would never have obtained the support it has
obtained from the people. It was the uniting of
the Land Question with the agitation for Home Rule
which really roused the peasantry. It is impossible
for any one who has not resided in Ireland, and
been on intimate terms with the people, to realize
the intense longing which animates them for the
possession of land, no matter how small or how bad
the holding may be. If a farm was vacant owing
to eviction of the tenant or otherwise, there were
always numbers ready to compete for it, and willing
to pay the landlord a fine for its possession, far
beyond its value. They would often borrow the
money to pay this fine at high interest, and, in
most cases, left themselves without sufficient means
to cultivate the land properly. To this land-hunger
was also due, to a great extent, the subdivision of
farms, which was so ruinous to the country; for
in former days the father of the family thought the
best way he could provide for his younger sons was
to give each of them some portion of his land. I
remember numbers of instances in our own immediate neighbourhood where farms, originally large,
were divided among the sons of the tenants, and
subsequently subdivided again and again, until some
of the holdings became quite too small to support
a family. In the neighbourhood of bogs these sub-

divisions were more numerous than in other places, the reason being that fuel was more easily and cheaply obtained there; in most cases, indeed, there were rights of turbary attached to the holdings.

This anxiety for the possession of land is no doubt, as has often been pointed out, largely due to the fact that Ireland is so destitute of mineral wealth, that there has been comparatively little industrial development, and that the land has been the only resource for the people; but I am sure that it is also an innate sentiment. Any one who once grasps the fact that this land-hunger does exist, and realizes at all what a passion it is, will easily see what an attraction there was for the peasantry in the hopes held out to them, that by joining this agitation they would ultimately get their land for little or nothing. These hopes were undoubtedly fostered by the Land Act of 1881, which, though it may have been unavoidable, certainly struck a fatal blow at the obligation of contract between landlord and tenant.

Hopes of this kind appeal with an especial force to an excitable and highly imaginative people like the Irish. It is scarcely possible to believe how extravagant are the hopes entertained by many of the peasantry of the benefits which they would derive from the establishment of an Irish Parliament. Not only do they expect that after a short time rent would be enormously reduced, or that they would become proprietors of their holdings at a very small price; but many of them have the most fanciful ideas as to the immediate advantages that would arise. Many believe that there are numerous mines and coal-fields which the English Government has never allowed to be worked, and that these would greatly enrich the country; while others suppose that wages would be at least trebled, and abundance of work afforded everywhere. In Dublin, too, there is a widespread idea that the city would be greatly benefited, as all the nobility and gentry would again reside there, as they did before the Union. In fact, it is no exaggeration to say that the peasantry at least expect that there would be "a plethora of wealth," and that "a pauper population would roll in riches." No reasonable man can doubt that all these hopes would be disappointed, except possibly that as to the land, which might indeed be realized, but only by a shameful and cruel injustice to the landlords; and the inevitable disappointment would, it can hardly be doubted, lead to a condition of discontent greater than any that has heretofore existed. I have always believed that it is the Land Question which is really at the root of the whole matter, and that it should be settled by some system of compulsory purchase to be determined upon and carried out by the Imperial Parliament, for it is difficult to imagine that such a question could be really fairly dealt with by a body of men elected almost entirely by the votes of one of the parties to the dispute.

Whatever may be said of the effect of the Union and of subsequent legislation, there is no doubt that the general condition of the country and the peasantry has improved in every respect during my lifetime. I cannot speak of the earlier days immediately following the Union; but I can clearly recollect what the country was over sixty years ago as compared with what it is now, and the improvement has been quite as great as the most sanguine could have expected.

I have already spoken of the faction fights which were common when I was a boy, and which have since entirely died out, although in some few places the recollection of the former feuds still exists, and is occasionally the cause of an isolated crime. A curious instance of this was mentioned in the Irish newspapers in September, 1893, an affray in which a man was killed during a football match at Cooga, in the county of Limerick, being attributed to the old ill-feeling between the "three-year-old" and "four-year-old" factions.

There have also, unfortunately, from time to time been serious outbreaks of crime, and there are some parts of the south where lawlessness still prevails to a lamentable extent; but, taking Ireland as a whole, there is no doubt that the peasantry have a greater respect for the law than they had in my early days, and that the country is more peaceful and quiet.

One feature which distinguished the outbreak of crime during the late land agitation from any that I remember, was that the outrages and intimidation were mainly directed, not against the landlords and agents as heretofore, but against any of the peasantry who broke or evaded the unwritten law of the Land League. It was marked by a far greater amount of combination than ever existed before, and it was by this combination that the taking of farms, from which tenants had for any cause been evicted, was so effectually prevented. It is not that the desire to take such farms is less than it ever was, but that no man dare take one, as he does so at the risk of his life.

Not long since, a tenant farmer, who punctually paid his rent, complained to me that two other tenants of the same landlord were allowed to hold their farms, although they were drunken, good-for-nothing fellows, and had for years paid no rent at all.

"Why should they be let stay there?" he asked indignantly.

"What possible advantage," I said, "could the landlord gain by evicting them? for neither you nor any of his other tenants would take the farms, nor would you" (for I knew he was a local leader of the League) "allow any one else to do so."

"Well," said he, with a sigh, "that's the law of the land."

I knew that if he dared he would have been only too glad to add these farms to the one he already had, for he was a hardworking and pushing man.

The drainage and cultivation of land have certainly greatly improved during my lifetime; and so have the dwellings of the peasantry. Large numbers of loans for drainage and other land improvements have been made by the Treasury through the Board of Public Works, and it is satisfactory to know that these loans have, on the whole, been advantageously expended and are being honestly repaid.

It is unfortunately true that considerable religious animosity still exists, which, though dormant, is ready to break out on any provocation; but I cannot see how these feelings would be at all mitigated by the proposed change in the government of this country; in fact, it appears to me that they would undoubtedly be intensified.

Looking back on the last seventy years, and remembering the progress that Ireland has made, I see no reason to despair of the future of my country. Although, during the first five and thirty years of my life, there was comparatively little change for the better in the condition of the people, since the year 1850 it has vastly improved. Wages have more than doubled; the people are better housed, better clad, and better fed. In recent years this improvement has been even more marked, and, if nothing untoward arises to retard its progress, if (is the hope too sanguine?) Ireland can cease to be "the battlefield of English parties," it will, I trust, ere many years, be as happy and contented as any part of our good Queen's dominions.

THE END.

www.ingramcontent.com/pod-product-compliance
Lightning Source LLC
Chambersburg PA
CBHW030748230426
43667CB00007B/892